Using Graphic Novels in the Science, Technology, Engineering, and Mathematics (STEM) Classroom

Using Graphic Novels in the Science, Technology, Engineering, and Mathematics (STEM) Classroom

WILLIAM BOERMAN-CORNELL,
JOSHA HO, DAVID KLANDERMAN,
AND SARAH KLANDERMAN

BLOOMSBURY ACADEMIC
LONDON • NEW YORK • OXFORD • NEW DELHI • SYDNEY

BLOOMSBURY ACADEMIC
Bloomsbury Publishing Plc
50 Bedford Square, London, WC1B 3DP, UK
1385 Broadway, New York, NY 10018, USA
29 Earlsfort Terrace, Dublin 2, Ireland

BLOOMSBURY, BLOOMSBURY ACADEMIC and the Diana logo are trademarks
of Bloomsbury Publishing Plc

First published in Great Britain 2024

Copyright © William Boerman-Cornell, Josha Ho, David Klanderman, and
Sarah Klanderman, 2024

William Boerman-Cornell, Josha Ho, David Klanderman, and Sarah Klanderman
have asserted their right under the Copyright, Designs and Patents Act, 1988,
to be identified as Authors of this work.

For legal purposes the Acknowledgments on pp. xii–xiv constitute an extension
of this copyright page.

Cover design: Grace Ridge
Cover image © Zoonar GmbH / Alamy Stock Photo and ~ Bitter ~ / Adobe Stock

Bloomsbury Publishing Plc does not have any control over, or responsibility for, any
third-party websites referred to or in this book. All internet addresses given in this
book were correct at the time of going to press. The author and publisher regret any
inconvenience caused if addresses have changed or sites have ceased to exist,
but can accept no responsibility for any such changes.

A catalogue record for this book is available from the British Library.

A catalog record for this book is available from the Library of Congress.

ISBN: HB: 978-1-3502-7919-3
PB: 978-1-3502-7918-6
ePDF: 978-1-3502-7921-6
eBook: 978-1-3502-7920-9

Typeset by Deanta Global Publishing Services, Chennai, India

To find out more about our authors and books visit www.bloomsbury.com and
sign up for our newsletters.

To all the amazing STEM teachers we have learned from—including Dr. Lawrence Fryling (who taught Bill middle school science and photography), Greg Dyck (Josha's high school chemistry teacher who introduced him to science comics), William Smout (Dave's AP chemistry teacher and Chess Team coach), and Teena Gerhardt (Sarah's inspirational math teacher)

CONTENTS

FIGURES

FOREWORD

Jay Hosler

Flying is not my favorite thing to do. While I understand the basic physics that allows a multi-ton tube of metal to get airborne, I am also intensely aware of the catastrophic ramifications that crashing can have on my biological systems. The evolutionary gift of imagination allows me to imagine the terror I would feel in the case of a crash. In the event of an emergency, I'm sure I would have trouble thinking straight as adrenaline and cortisol surge into my bloodstream, increasing my heart rate and interfering with my short-term memory storage. Which makes the airline's crash instructions all the more interesting. What is it that they provide in this moment of intense stress? How do they communicate critical information when it is literally a matter of life and death?

They use comics.

Most of the crash instructions that I have seen are laid out in a sequence of images that explain important procedures in a chronological, stepwise fashion. Airlines turn to comics when they need to convey important information quickly and effectively and, if they use text at all, it is very limited. Why would they do that? Because comics are a great way to learn something.

This may sound counterintuitive to some folks. We live in a culture that routinely mocks a person's intelligence if they read "books with pictures." But as an academic biologist, I consider books with pictures to be the norm. Textbooks have blossomed into unwieldy tomes that are richly illustrated with color images and diagrams. Research articles in the sciences use textual explanations, data figures, diagrams, and models to explain complex new ideas. The truth is, scientists have relied on images and stories to explain monumental shifts in our understanding of the natural world for centuries. Charles Darwin's branching tree was a radical reimagining of how life on earth may have evolved. Santiago Ramon y Cajal's images of the nervous system are masterpieces that not only have hung in art museums but have also fundamentally changed our understanding of how the brain works. Einstein used a simple image and a story about a train to explain his special theory of relativity.

If images were all comics had to offer, it would be a lot. But the possibilities comics offer extend far beyond just being a richly illustrated textbook.

The best science comics use narratives and characters to draw us into the experience of learning. They help forge an emotional connection between the reader and the material in a way that textbooks cannot. This emotional connection is one that is often neglected in science communication and instruction. We focus so much on the elegant experiments designed to peel back the mysteries of nature, that we forget to notice the passionate, deeply human scientists doing the work. We sometimes shy away from sharing this wonder because we want the work to stand for itself. Unfortunately, isolated facts are only exciting to a rarefied few who already appreciate the beauty of a system. Most need us to show them the wonder. Comics can do this like no other medium.

While textbooks present images and text together, they are separated spatially. A reader must pop out of the text when prompted to look at a graph or data chart. Comics can blend these elements seamlessly, drawing readers through a story and passing through figures and diagrams that are part of the narrative. Comics allow us to experience discovery through the eyes of characters, to see them ask the same questions we have, and to visualize complex processes as part of one unified story. The following Stephen Jay Gould quote has been a guiding principle for the natural science comics I create.

> We cannot win this battle to save species and environments without forging an emotional bond between ourselves and nature as well—for we will not fight to save what we do not love.

Comics do this. They let us see the world from alien points of view and provide stories that can show us the consequences of major problems like global warming. When they use stories, comics tap into our species' predisposition to narrative explanations and provide essential scaffolding for big scientific ideas. Unlike video, comics allow readers to control the flow of information and force them to actively use their imaginations to connect images and construct mental models. And, like the picture books we read early in life, they provide visual and context clues for new terms and concepts.

Using Graphic Novels in the Science, Technology, Engineering, and Mathematics (STEM) Classroom provides an essential guide to the world of science comics and their potential as a powerful mechanism to engage and excite students. In these pages, Bill Boerman-Cornell, Sarah Klanderman, Dave Klanderman, and Josha Ho lay out a lucid argument for using comics in a science classroom and provide examples to help you get started. Critically, they illustrate student successes and feedback and provide advice for teachers who may know nothing about comics but want to give them a try. I am grateful to have this book in the world so I can share it with the teachers I hear from who need something to help them get a foothold. But, as you will soon see, this book offers much more than just a foothold. It's a full set of climbing gear.

It would be wrong to read my enthusiasm for science comics as a call to replace all textbooks. However, I would like to suggest that comics can do something textbooks rarely do. Comics have the power to unify three creative aspects of human imagination that have been artificially separated over the years. When my kids were young, the boundaries between science, story, and art did not exist. Experiments were part of stories they told themselves and were illustrated in crayon. But when they started school, we separated those things. Art was in one room, science in another, and reading was in yet another. Imagine a medium that crumbles those borders and allows a broader expression of a student's creativity. Imagine a system that lets an artistically inclined student visualize models to better understand a complicated system, or supports a natural-born storyteller to deploy their explanatory and entertainment skills to trick us into learning something. Now imagine those students working together. Or, better yet, imagine we helped each student cultivate all of these creative skills in the pursuit of understanding. Comics provide a model for that type of thinking. They show students how they can engage with science in ways they never expected.

Jay Hosler has a Ph.D. in biological sciences from the University of Notre Dame. He holds the David K. Goodman Endowed Chair in Biology at Juniata College in Pennsylvania where he is a full professor and chair of the Biology Department. He is the creator of some of the best science graphic novels ever, including *Clan Apis*, recently re-released as *The Way of the Hive* and *Santiago!*, a biography of artist, scientist, and troublemaker Santiago Ramon y Cajal. But, honestly, all of his books are really good. You should buy them right now. The authors of this book believe that Hosler has the superpower of telepathic communication with bees, beetles, and all insect life.

ACKNOWLEDGMENTS

This book is a clear demonstration about how learning and writing about science, technology, engineering, and math depends upon a community of generous people who are willing to share knowledge and ideas. These people strengthened this book a great deal and deserve credit for it. Any errors which remain are in spite of their good work.

Thank you to Tatsuji Ebihara, Monica Crinion, and Willem Mouw—all three of them excellent engineers who were willing to be interviewed about how they interact with literacy in their good work. Thank you to our peer reviewers: Joseph Slawinski (amazing high school science teacher), Dr. Michael Bosscher (elementally remarkable Professor of Chemistry), Dr. Clay Carlson (highly adaptable Professor of Biology), Dr. Tatsuji Ebihara (outstandingly creative engineer), Dr. Valorie Zonnefeld, (unequaled Professor of Mathematics), and Samuel Hofman (one of Dave's amazing Math Education students) who provided factual corrections, wording suggestions, and encouragement. We are also thankful for the anonymous peer reviewers that our editor lined up for us.

On that note, we are thankful for our amazing editor, Maria Brauzzi, who has been our ambassador to the publishing world and a friend across the ocean. We are also thankful for her assistant, Laura Gallon, who stepped in when Maria was busy bringing a child into the world. We are also thankful for the designers, producers, and lots of other people at Bloomsbury who made this book a reality.

Jay Hosler wrote an amazing foreword on short notice during a busy part of the semester. We are grateful for that. But we are even more grateful for the skill and expertise he brings to writing the best science graphic novels out there. While we are at it, our thanks to all the other graphic novel creators who have chosen to write about science, engineering, technology, and math. Thank you for your beautiful, thought-provoking work that does so much to bring STEM understanding to a larger audience.

There were several teachers who tried out some graphic novels and informed us of the results. Our thanks to Ben Gliesmann, who is a former student of two of the authors and teaches middle school for the Chicago Public Schools (and we are proud of him); Dr. Jim Turner, who is an amazing math professor, and Dr. Jason Ho, who is a fantastic physics professor.

Sarah would like to thank Josha Ho for entertaining their glee toward graphic novels and bringing new light into what chaos entropy can bring.

She would also like to thank her wonderful geometry students, especially Alexis, Coin, Flynn, Nolan, and Sophie (you know who you are even with the pseudonyms) for your insightful feedback. She can't wait to hear about the ways in which they will be using graphic novels in their own teaching.

Josha would like to thank Stefan Popowycz and Nihar Dalmia, and his whole information design family who taught him everything about marrying quantitative research with qualitative. He would also like to thank Sarah Klanderman for being who she is.

Dave thanks his children and their spouses for positive suggestions and loving support, especially Sarah and Josha, co-authors of this book, for their collaboration and insightful comments. He continues to be inspired by the thousands of students he has been privileged to teach for over thirty-five years (including multiple generations and many who are now themselves teachers). Dave thanks Bill Boerman-Cornell for his leadership, creativity, and positive attitude during the process of writing this book. Dave would like to acknowledge the support of Calvin University for providing the time necessary to complete work for this book, including a sabbatical during the 2022–3 academic year. Finally, Dave would like to thank his wife and best friend for over three decades, Barbara. She has provided a listening ear, encouragement during difficult moments, and helpful suggestions along the way.

Bill is grateful for Dave, Sarah, and Josha who were willing to undertake this project with excitement and were gentle in correcting Bill when his amateur understanding of the STEM fields was showing. Bill is also grateful to Chicago Semester for granting him a Scholar-in-Residence fellowship which allowed him time to work on this book. Bill's colleagues at Trinity were understanding when his looming deadline got in the way of some other projects. Thank you Dr. Christine Scholma, Dr. Michael Dieter, and the whole STAT Project team.

Marissa Moss, author and publisher extraordinaire has been a friend and mentor to Bill for a while. He is grateful for her help with permissions and her wisdom.

Finally, there are some people in Bill's life that have supported him in a variety of ways. He is grateful, as always, for the friendship of John Bekker, Rick Veen, and Chris Wolterstorff as well as the Chi 35 group. His brothers Tom and Mike, both excellent teachers, have influenced his thinking about education and the rest of the world. Bill is also thankful for his parents who encouraged his love of reading and didn't discourage his love of comic books—at least not too much. Bill and his family share a house with Rob and Mary Lagerwey and their family. We are grateful for the chance to live in community with them.

Finally, Bill is grateful for his children, Kathryn, Frances, and Willem. They have grown into wonderful adults who he likes to spend time with. And Bill is married to an amazing fourth-grade teacher who keeps him grounded and supported. Thank you, Amy, for being in my life. I promise I will come up from the basement study now.

CHAPTER 1

What Research Tells Us about Using Graphic Novels to Teach Science, Technology, Engineering, and Mathematics

Teaching science, technology, engineering, and mathematics is not always easy. While students' wonder and curiosity about the world seem limitless when they are young, as the demand ratchets up in fourth or fifth grade, it becomes harder for them to look at the world with the same degree of wonder and curiosity. Along with the increased demand on their learning and loss of awe and amazement often comes a resistance to learning and sometimes a negative perception of math and science.

Before we can blame students, though, we have to acknowledge that with each succeeding year, students need to learn ever-increasing amounts of material, procedure, and concepts. Among the things middle school and high school students will need to learn in science, technology, engineering and mathematics (STEM) fields are (to name only a few): the conceptual language of precision measurement; investigation and problem-solving through experimentation; breaking down problems into smaller pieces through analysis; reassembling those same pieces through synthesis; how equations translate to real-life applications; and the connections between numbers, diagrams, and concepts. While many amazing STEM teachers manage to keep curiosity and even enthusiasm alive in their students, district-wide emphases on test scores over learning, overloaded curricula, poorly written or out-of-date textbooks, and lack of time and resources for real investigation and authentic problem-solving certainly don't make it easy.

Graphic Novels May Be Able to Help

Graphic novels are increasingly being incorporated into STEM classrooms. The way that graphic novels combine images and text makes them particularly well-suited for STEM instruction by helping students visualize and understand abstract or overarching concepts and connect those concepts to real-world applications. Graphic novels use a system of sequenced panels, text boxes, and word/thought balloons to make abstract concepts concrete and to bring real-world applications to life in the classroom.

To understand genetics, for example, one needs to be able to visualize how DNA and RNA proteins work together, how dominant and recessive genes and epigenetics influence biological traits, and how natural selection modifies organisms over time. A textbook can describe these processes in the primary textual flow (the column of words that students follow from page to page) and in isolated sidebars, photographs, charts, diagrams, and illustrations. Unfortunately, students tend to skip the sidebars in their reading or look at them separately from the concepts being described in the primary textual flow. And in the case of genetics, trying to understand the concepts and processes involved by reading only text without thinking about the visuals that accompany them, is, at best, very difficult. This is driven by many of the same human limitations that reading graphs with legends have. As Edward Tufte states in *The Visual Display of Quantitative Information,* "Viewers need the help that words can provide . . . to integrate the caption and legend [of a graphic] into the design so that the eye is not required to dart back and forth between textual material and the graphic" (2001, p. 180). Likewise, a student skimming through the text and looking only at photographs, charts, and graphic depictions of processes, will likely miss the big picture of how everything fits together—which the primary textual flow provides.

Graphic novels combine the two in a way that makes the chart or diagram an intrinsic part of the textual flow. And because what is in a graphic novel is limited only by a creator's knowledge, skill, and imagination, graphic novels can display images and special effects out of reach for science-based films.

Consider this image from Schultz, Cannon, and Cannon's graphic novel, *The Stuff of Life: A Graphic Guide to Genetics and DNA* (2009, p. 33) (Figure 1.1).

In this graphic novel, an alien race of creatures that look like sea cucumbers and reproduce by fission is suffering from genetic destabilization and sends a scientist to spy on Earth to learn how genetics work there. On page thirty-three, the first two panels show part of that story, as the leader of the alien civilization asks the scientist for clarification of a point of his explanation. Then in the following four panels we get a visual analogy of a zipper applied to one part of DNA replication; then a series of images that contextualize how DNA is part of a chromosome which is part of the

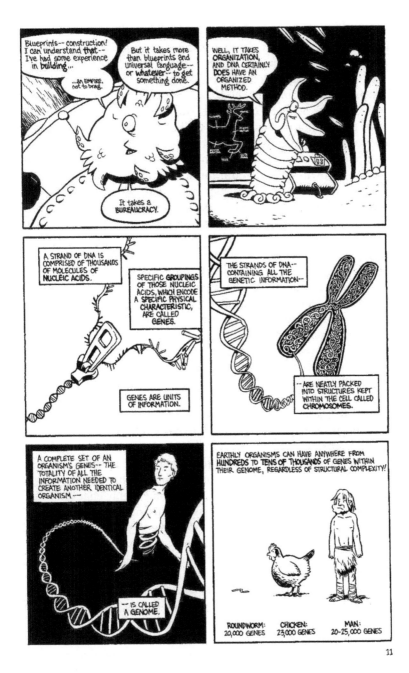

FIGURE 1.1 *A page excerpt explaining DNA replication within* The Stuff of Life: A Graphic Guide to Genetics and DNA (2009, p.33).

encoding system for human characteristics, and finally the characteristics of all animals. That is a lot of clearly explained conceptual information in just six panels. Further, a deeply compelling story that integrates visuals with text can connect effectively to differently motivated students.

This particular example image is, as of this writing, over a decade old, and may no longer be perfectly consistent with contemporary science regarding the way genes influence traits. But while a textbook is swiftly outdated because of the tendency to confidently assert data interpretations as fact, the nature of this narrative—an alien trying to figure out a genetic system that is not his own—allows room for a nuanced discussion about how, as new data becomes available, science takes that into account. Because the very format of a graphic novel is less authoritative—it looks more like a cartoon than a textbook—students may have an easier time questioning the ideas that they find there. As a secondary benefit of this graphic novel, for example, this questioning of ideas is one of the most important skills we can teach students. Those students that go on to a career in the sciences will need that questioning in order to make new discoveries and to find new approaches. Students who might not become scientists will still benefit from the critical approach that science provides, both in how they look at news reports about scientific studies and in practically all other parts of their lives.

In this book we do not suggest that graphic novels should replace textbooks, but rather that they can complement them. Further, we do not suggest that graphic novels replace direct instruction, analogies, humor, YouTube videos, diagrams, problem sets, hands-on experimentation, reciprocal instruction, required written explanations, reading from trade books (unlike textbooks, trade books are written for the general public and sold in bookstores), demonstrations, and other inventive approaches. These are all important and versatile tools that can be used to supplement regular instruction, remediate struggling readers, and capture the excitement for further knowledge in students who have become highly engaged in a topic. In the chapters to come we will discuss how to incorporate graphic novels as subjects of whole class study, as supplementary texts to help students struggling with concepts, and as supplemental texts for students who want to extend their understanding. Sometimes that will mean reading the entire book, sometimes excerpts. In short, we are suggesting that graphic novels are yet another tool to allow teachers to reach the specific goals that they have for their students in relation to the academic discipline that they teach.

Graphic novels can allow students to read an explanation multiple times, to see the causal results of manipulating variables, and can even challenge them to work out coding, math, engineering, and experimental problems for themselves. Graphic novels can be an engaging basis for classroom discussion that allows students to interact with multiple chapters at once, unlike trying to sync up portions of a YouTube video. Graphic novels will not always result in students being instantly excited about science and math—but they can help bridge a student's attention from something they are excited about to a STEM subject that connects to their interests in ways they never considered. Graphic novels can make a difference for your students.

We have an entire book to consider those claims, but let's start with what research can tell us about the effectiveness of teaching with graphic novels. And before we do that, let's make sure we know what we are referring to when we talk about graphic novels.

What Is a Graphic Novel?

Before we have a look at the studies that examine how graphic novels help students develop these skills, we should take a moment to explain how most of the research we will be citing defines what a graphic novel is and what it isn't. This book, along with most graphic novel research, defines graphic novels as book-length, self-contained narratives that use the conventions of a comic book to present information. Some comic book creators, teachers, and researchers prefer other terms, like *comics*, *graphica*, or *sequential art*. They argue that the term *graphic novel* is pretentious or inaccurate. We readily acknowledge that the term *graphic novel* is not ideal. Graphic novels are not solely graphic (since they consist not only of graphics but words too). And graphic novels are not always novels either. Usually, the term *novel* is used to refer to a fictional story in book form. Graphic novels, however, can be biographies, nonfiction explorations of a particular topic, reports, textbooks, and other nonfiction forms.

We would argue, though, that the term *graphic novel* allows us to make some important distinctions. The terms *comic* and *comic book* imply a relatively short, side-stapled product of the sort you might buy at a grocery store or specialty shop. The content of a comic often concerns superheroes and is usually presented in serial form, with some stories continuing for years and even decades (Spider-Man, the Avengers, and the X-Men's storylines began in the 1960s, and Superman and Batman even further back than that). While such stories are both popular and enjoyable, their serial format and particular genres are not always easy to connect with STEM curricula. The term also has other meanings like short one-to-six panel comic strips like *Calvin and Hobbes, Zits, The Boondocks*, or *Foxtrot*. And the term *comics* also implies that the format is, by nature, humorous.

Graphica is an overarching term, one that includes comics, graphic novels, wordless paneled narratives, and sometimes picture books or other formats that separate the images from the words. So while the term *comics* is too narrow for our scope, the term *graphica* is too wide. All graphic novels are graphica, not all graphica are graphic novels.

Finally, some graphic novels might self-identify as cartoons and their creators as cartoonists. This term, however, tends to get conflated with the definition of cartoons as animated programs like *Sponge Bob Square Pants* or *The Simpsons.*

So we will distinguish graphic novels from comics, graphica, or cartoons. Our definition for these purposes is that a graphic novel is any book-length narrative, fiction or nonfiction, that uses panels, word balloons, and other conventions of a comic book. With our terms defined, we will now examine particular findings of research into the value of using graphic novels in the classroom.

What Can Graphic Novels Do for Teaching and Learning in General?

Research about the educational value of graphic novels is only about twenty years old, and there is still a great deal that we have to learn. However, the studies undertaken so far are painting a clearer and clearer picture of the affordances and constraints of graphic novels in the classroom. The research so far is compatible with a more general finding that achievement in reading and writing is correlated with success in college science and mathematics courses of study.

To begin with, multiple studies have shown that the way that graphic novels combine images and words to convey information results in more engagement and more thorough comprehension for many students across disciplinary lines. This evidence is of particular interest to STEM instruction because, as we mentioned earlier in this chapter, science, technology, engineering, and mathematics all require students to develop the ability to combine information from words with information from charts, figures, tables, diagrams, and other visual ways of understanding. Graphic novels embed the textual flow and images together in an ordered sequence of panels—much like the way a teacher talks through an image verbally while pointing to information on the graphic (e.g., on a smart board) at the same time.

Graphic Novels Increase Reading Comprehension

On the most basic of levels, teachers of any discipline want students to comprehend concepts, ideas, and content that they are teaching. As we shall see, there is a strong collection of studies that show that graphic novels increase student comprehension. These studies have come at the question of comprehension from a wide range of angles.

Several studies have looked at high school comprehension levels. Cook (2014) did an experimental study with 217 high school students. He compared students reading graphic novels with conventional texts containing the same information and found that the grade level and gender of the reader have a significant effect on how well students learn from graphic novels (though that may have been because there were a smaller range of graphic novels available at the time, and fewer of them were written by women). Meyer and Jimenez (2017) compared an experienced graphic novel reader with a novice graphic novel reader and found that teaching both types of readers a particular model for learning graphic novel reading skills had a positive effect on comprehension. Wood (2015) and Lim (2019) also saw increased comprehension skills in high school students that read graphic novels.

Higher comprehension results are not confined to just English-speaking countries either. Oz and Efecioglu (2015) looked at English language learners in two Turkish tenth-grade classes. Using questionnaires, semi-structured interviews, and post-tests, they found that graphic novels increased scores in symbol recognition, setting recognition, and ability to identify foreshadowing. Wong, Miao, Cheng, and Yip (2017) found similar improved comprehension among Chinese high school students, and Aldahash and Altahab (2020) saw increased reading comprehension with graphic novels in Saudi Arabia. While different cultures tend to develop a distinct artistic style, the basic conventions of a graphic novel (panel layout, word balloons, panel-to-panel transitions, etc.) remain constant to a large extent across geographic and political boundaries, and so this research is, at least to an extent, generalizable.

Teaching STEM puts a heavy demand upon student comprehension. The evidence points toward the idea that the words, the images, and the interaction between the words and images constitute three separate contexts to support reading comprehension for students. In addition, multiple studies, using a range of observational and self-reporting measures, (Arnett, 2008; Moeller 2008, 2011; Gavigan 2010, 2011; Gomes & Carter 2010) have found that graphic novels engage student interest effectively. The study of graphic novels is still a young subset of literacy research and there are no meta-analyses yet, and while it is certainly true that different learning styles, ability levels, and types of cognition will have different results in terms of comprehension and motivation, the evidence is overwhelming that student readers as a whole comprehend better when reading graphic novels.

Graphic Novels Develop Critical Thinking Skills

Seldom does a week go by without another newsfeed headline proclaiming that a study has determined that a glass of wine every night is good for your heart, or that a glass of wine every night is not good for your heart. One study proclaims that flossing helps your teeth, another disagrees. If one reads the articles that follow the headlines, it often becomes clear that the headline is an inadequate summary of the results of the study. Newspaper summaries of scientific studies seldom explain the methodology or results of the study, and so the readers are left with only an overly simplistic headline and a brief summary that is long on implications and short on limitations of the study. And if one looks up and reads the original research paper, one often finds that the study is not saying what the headline implies at all.

Similar summaries accompany news reports (and social media posts) regarding a wide array of social, environmental, and policy challenges. The future of our world quite literally depends on teaching students to be able to read and understand the information that science, engineering, and mathematics put before us, and that technology disseminates. Quantitative literacy and data comprehension have become necessary components of being an informed citizen of any country. Increasingly, STEM teachers are expected to teach not only the particulars of the methodology and content of their discipline but also how to interpret scientific and statistical results in a bewildering array of contexts. Limited class time and overwhelming content to be covered may make such instruction difficult, but graphic novels may be able to help students to learn to think critically about climate change, how to respond to pandemics, conspiracy theories, the effects of social media, and other important and complex issues.

Teaching students to think critically is complicated and researching critical thinking is likewise many-faceted. To start with, the reading process of graphic novels is complicated. Although many people believe that graphic novels are easier to read than regular books, in fact, reading graphic novels well is a very complex activity. Monnin (2008) identified multiple levels of word and image literacies that student readers had to negotiate to read the graphic novel *Bone*. As we have already mentioned in this chapter, comprehending graphic novels requires drawing information not only from the text and the images but also from the interaction between the two.

Chun (2009) and Hammond (2011) both used single texts (*Maus* and *American Born Chinese* respectively) and found that both works helped students develop critical literacy skills. Boerman-Cornell (2013) conducted a content analysis and found that the combination of text and image in George O'Connor's *Journey into Mohawk Country* could be used to teach irony and critical thinking. Sabeti (2012) conducted semi-structured interviews with ten students and identified varying levels of critical reading in three different contexts of reading graphic novels: in school, in extracurricular reading groups, and at home. Snow and Robbins (2015) found that students studying graphic novels looked for factual errors and biased perspectives, using critical literacy skills. Groenke and Savitz (2016) interviewed students and teachers and concluded that reading engagement, " . . . does not need to be separate from the sophisticated, critical thinking we want readers to do with texts." (n.p.). Each of these studies contributes to the overall impression that graphic novels hold many affordances for teaching students to think critically about the material presented.

Critical thinking is a skill that serves STEM students well. Graphic novels offer opportunities to develop those skills (particularly in conjunction with STEM-based graphic novels, which we will discuss later in this book).

Graphic Novels Develop Cultural Understanding

Cultural understanding seems like it might be the province of humanities subjects like English and Social Studies. STEM subjects, after all, deal with objectively measurable data. Traditionally, it doesn't matter who discovers the theorem, solves the problem, develops and supports the theory, designs the structure, makes the observations, runs the experiment, or writes the code. Some teachers will say that it isn't the culture of the scientist, programmer, engineer, or mathematician that matters, rather it is the facts, numbers, and results.

However, for students first encountering the STEM fields in a serious way and considering how STEM will become part of their lives (either as a career, or just by being an informed citizen who understands how science works), it does matter. Students need to know that there are women who are scientists and people of color who are scientists. Students need to know that science is a way of seeing the world that can be helpful for economically needy communities rather than just corporations, governments, or upper middle-class people. In short, when teaching science, culture does matter. It matters a great deal. Graphic novels can help students effectively consider culture in science.

Scholars began by considering possible affordances that graphic novels might offer to help students consider cultural understanding. Vandermeersche and Soetaert (2011) laid the theoretical groundwork for how graphic novels could function effectively as mediating texts to lead into discussions about culture. Royal (2012) described how graphic novels dealt with cultural and racial perceptions and stereotypes. These studies argued that graphic novels at least theoretically have potential.

Later studies considered data more closely. Hughes and Morrison (2014) engaged in discourse analysis of a school-based book club discussion. The book club specifically considered graphic novels that explored the indigenous experience. They found, " . . . that these texts have been excellent classroom tools with which to build cultural awareness and with which to explore different social, political, and economic issues" (p. 125). Stephens (2015) analyzed the responses from two freshman English classes after reading a graphic novel and found that their dominant cultures acted as filters, determining what they would notice and what they did not notice. Calling students' attention to this observation could help them understand that different people see the world through different lenses and that empathy is sometimes necessary to understand other people's perspectives.

Most STEM teachers would agree that what is observed or not observed shapes our interpretations of the world. Helping students connect the culture in which they find their identity to the culture of STEM classes and studies makes it easier to welcome all students into fuller participation in science, technology, engineering, and math classes so that they can bring that understanding into all the cultures they participate in. Later chapters will describe specific graphic novels that help build cultural understanding in students.

Graphic Novels Develop Multimodal Literacy Skills

Earlier in this chapter, we spoke of the way in which most STEM content requires students to be able to interpret information from both text and visuals, often charts and diagrams. Literacy researchers refer to that sort of reading as *multimodal*. People take in information multimodally any time they are on social media, driving on a highway with billboards, or whenever they read a magazine in a waiting room. Graphic novels are a particular type of multi-modality which, rather than the text being below or above or beside the image, features the text and image occupying the same space. Consequently, when students read graphic novels, they practice learning to read with an eye toward pulling information from both image and text (and the interaction between the two). At the same time, because students have grown up reading multimodally, the graphic format may be one that feels comfortable to them.

Research confirms that reading graphic novels develops skills in multimodal interpretation. Hammond (2009) observed twenty-three twelfth-grade students reading graphic novels and saw increased multimodal literacy skills. Conners (2010) conducted a case study of six high school students and found that through reading graphic novels, they developed appropriate strategies for reading multimodally. Hughes, King, Perkins, and Fuke (2011), Conners (2012), and Gillenwater (2014) all found similar results. Graphic novels are a good way to help students learn the practices and habits of understanding the intersection of images and texts.

Graphic Novels Improve Written Communication Skills

Too often people fall into thinking of STEM subjects being all about numbers while words are the province of disciplines like history and language arts. Since there are numbers involved in math and science and words involved in historical accounts and narrative writing, the common unexamined assumption is that number systems and word systems are two mutually exclusive systems.

Of course, this is not true. Science requires observations, and observations require verbal descriptions as well as data tables and graphs. Computer coding involves being able to write in languages that draw upon words and numbers in ways that utterly depend upon both. Engineers need not only be able to work with equations to be able to construct things, but they also need to be able to use writing to translate understanding to architects, builders, and other engineers. Similarly, while mathematics is certainly a language that uses numbers and variables, writing allows mathematicians to share ideas, challenges, equations, problems, and discoveries, and most pure mathematics research has no numbers in it at all! And participation in all STEM fields involves extensive interaction with colleagues, clients, students, and others. Because of the stakes (bridges that are safe to drive on, encryption systems that protect digital bank accounts, medical experimentation that confirms the safety of drugs that could change people's lives, etc.) communication skills are vital in the STEM fields.

Using graphic novels to build writing proficiency is an area of graphic novel research that is still under development. Frey and Fisher (2004) wrote one of the first studies to suggest that reading graphic novels improved not only reading skills, but writing skills as well. In several studies and anecdotal reports which followed, researchers and practitioners alike suggested having students write their own graphic novels. Those studies praised student engagement and self-expression while saying little about how this would help them develop writing skills. Further, without extensive training in layout, drawing, graphic novel script writing, coloring, and lettering, it is questionable whether what students produce helps them to grow in writing skills, image-building skills, or integrating the two.

More recent and more solid research suggests directions for future research and hints at the potential that graphic novels might hold. Akbar (2019) tested the value of using comic strips as a mentor text to teach seventy-five high school seniors in Indonesia to write narratives and used a pre- and post-test model to see if there was progress. Mentor texts are simply texts that serve as examples to show students how to write in terms of point-of-view, narrative movement, description, and so on, without necessarily requiring that students write in the same format. There was significant improvement with 78.5 percent of students in class achieving the target score. Although as we pointed out earlier, comic strips are not the same as graphic novels, the potential that Akbar's study shows for comic strips on a micro level can perhaps be generalized to the longer narratives of graphic novels as well.

Degracia (2012) studied the use of a nonfiction graphic novel memoir called *Stitches* (Small 2009) to teach students to write their own memoirs. Degracia uses this powerful text as an exemplar without requiring students to respond by creating their own graphic novel, but by encouraging them to write their own memoir with regular text. She has seen positive results in terms of subjectively strong narratives. But while this research is encouraging, there is a great deal of work that needs to be done before we can say definitively that graphic novels are helpful for teaching writing.

Of course, the skills described on the proceeding pages are all general skills. While they apply to some degree or another to teaching in the STEM fields, they are not skills that are particular to a specific discipline. There has, however, been additional research done about the effectiveness of graphic novels within the STEM disciplines.

Graphic Novels Are Useful for Teaching Science

Jetton and Shanahan (2012) identify several curricular goals for each academic discipline that are necessary for students to achieve if they are going to be literate in that field. They are quick to point out, however, that it is not reasonable to treat science as being monolithic. Even within the subject of biology, what is necessary to understand how to read genetics is very different from what is necessary to understand in order to read about animal behavior. In the realm of physics, astrophysics requires students to think differently in some ways than fluid dynamics does. However, there are some aspects of communicating in science that are universal, according to Jetton and Shanahan. The vocabulary includes scientific terminology that students must learn not only in terms of definitions but also in terms of the concepts behind those definitions. Students must distinguish the ways that different subfields of science might use the same words in different ways. Comprehension in science also requires students to be able to think about concepts represented graphically through charts or graphs.

Jetton and Shanahan further point out that scientists need to know how to read different sorts of material and documents than other fields do. These documents include:

- Raw data

- Field notes or logs

- Refereed journal articles

- Personal communications such as interviews, letters, emails, and conversations (p. 162)

So, can graphic novels help students read and think like a scientist? What does the research say? In 2009, Tatalovic summarized earlier research on using comic books and single-panel cartoons to teach science, but also referenced some of the earliest science-based graphic novels like Jay Hosler's *Clan Apis* (originally published in 1998 and recently re-released as

The Way of the Hive by HarperCollins) and Jim Ottaviani's *Suspended in Language* (first published in 2004 with a second edition released in 2009). Tatlovic concludes that graphic novels may well have even more potential for teaching science than one-panel cartoons and comic strips do, but also calls for more research in this area that is specific to science.

Nesmith, Cooper and Schwarz (2011) conducted focus groups for eleven elementary teachers and four college professors about their experience with and interest in using graphic novels to teach science. While Nesmith et al. were looking at attitudes more than classroom practice, what they found is certainly interesting. The teachers they surveyed recognized the potential benefits of graphic novels with the initial list focusing more on general learning than science-based learning. The science teachers noted that graphic novels attract student interest across a wide range of readers and ethnicities and that the writing style of graphic novels was relatable.

When, in the same study, Nesmith et al. dug a bit deeper in a second round of questions, there were more science-specific advantages that teachers and professors perceived in using graphic novels: graphic novels lead to higher-order thinking, contain realistic connections and examples, include real-world activities, introduce or reinforce important concepts, and provide good visuals to support content. Research subjects also identified some concerns. Some graphic novels are inaccurate, contain too few examples, and are not sufficient on their own but need to be combined with a more comprehensive text. They also expressed concern that parents would perceive graphic novels as too simple or dumbed-down to be effective tools for learning.

Brozo and Mayville (2012) took field notes on a middle school science class that was using graphic novels. They found that students responded enthusiastically, that the graphic novels helped students learn science vocabulary, and that the images helped them to learn the concepts behind the vocabulary in greater depth. In a later paper, Brozo (2015) conducted a case study of an eighth-grade teacher and students using the graphic novel *Genome* as a course text. Brozo found that the graphic novel stimulated interest and involvement in lessons, increased learning of essential information, and developed interpretive and critical thinking. Both of these studies, however, were not focused on looking at the particular demands and goals of a science class, but rather determining whether the general skills observed in other contexts would also work in a science classroom. The research seemed to show that it would.

Similarly, we can examine studies looking at the effectiveness of graphic novels for conveying information about medicine and health. Like Brozo's work, much of this research looked at whether observations of general skills also applied to teaching aspects of the science of medicine. Albright and Gavigan (2014) used pre- and post-surveys and focus groups to consider the effect of reading a health-based graphic novel on forty fifteen-to-twenty-year-olds (and in the later study, 142 young adults). The first study found that "After reading the graphic novel, there was a 25% decrease in the number of people who believed that HIV/AIDS was transmitted genetically. There were smaller results for other debunked facts" (p. 182). This is particularly interesting research in a world where the conclusions that science offers about global climate change, recommended practices and treatments for global pandemics, and other topics are often conflated with rumor, misinformation, and conspiracy theories.

Another study found similar results and concluded that graphic novels can be an effective HIV/AIDS prevention tool for young adults. Lo-Fo-Wong, Beijaerts, deHaes, and Sprangers (2014) looked at cancer, not in terms of education for prevention, but in terms of providing emotional empathy and support. They conducted a content analysis of Marisa Acocella Marchetto's graphic novel *Cancer Vixen*, to determine what affordances and constraints graphic novels like this might offer science teachers. Their analysis showed " . . . that the graphic novel depicts the full range of [cancer-related] distress by portraying practical, social, emotional, religious, spiritual, and physical problems" (p. 1554).

Another focus of research is what graphic novels can offer to aid science instruction. Boerman-Cornell, Kim, and Manderino (2017) identify three habits of thinking associated with science: Questioning, Hypothesizing, and Model Building. They also identify three habits of practice in science: Constructing Models of Scientific Processes; Writing Scientific Explanations; and Reading Nonlinguistic Scientific Representations. They go on to give examples of graphic novels that demonstrate each of these habits.

Meier (2012) used content analysis to investigate the same question, also identifying two specific affordances that science graphic novels can provide teachers. First, embedding pictures in text can encourage students to engage more deeply in the research questions and scientific concepts (and not merely stick to the primary textual flow, skipping over graphs and illustrations). Second, anthropomorphizing objects of study (whether strings of molecules or honeybees) can help students connect with difficult conceptual material. These specific approaches to explanation, common in STEM-focused graphic novels, can help students visualize and understand concepts that are hard to observe.

Finally, Jee and Anggoro (2012) draw on research from cognitive psychology and education theory to propose a series of ways in which the graphic novel format might be able to offer affordances for teaching science. They identify four cognitive impacts from their analysis that graphic novels: " . . . make scientific concepts and principles more concrete" (p. 199); " . . . capitalize on the benefits of spatially contiguous text and images" (p. 199); " . . . invoke schemas that influence comprehension" (p. 200); and " . . . influence metacognitive judgments about science understanding" (p. 201).

While these are excellent ideas about how graphic novels can help reach disciplinary goals in science, they are often defining further questions that need additional, more empirical research. Yet this work can only take place when science teachers, confident in the body of research that substantiates the value of graphic novels in the classroom, begin experimenting with them more widely.

Can Graphic Novels Be Helpful in Teaching Technology and Engineering?

We could find no studies that looked at using graphic novels in the context of a technology or an engineering classroom. Wolsey, Lapp, Grant, and Karkouti (2019) analyzed a discussion with an engineer about what is important for engineers to know in terms of oral and written communication. The engineer is quoted in the article as saying:

> Procedures can be forgotten, but if you understand where to go for the procedure and you understand foundationally why you are trying to solve a problem, you're more likely to remember it and be able to communicate it to your team. Communication for engineers happens through talking and sharing written ideas. (p. 251)

Wolsey et al. further point out that our goal as teachers is not necessarily to teach students to talk and think like professional engineers. At the same time, though, every high school student could benefit from learning the process of solving a physically anchored problem.

While there are not yet any studies that look specifically at the efficacy of graphic novels to teach engineering, we have shown over the last several pages that extensive research has supported the notion that graphic novels can help reach a remarkable range of different academic disciplines' overall curricular goals. In both the technology and engineering chapters that follow, we will attempt to remedy this by including research on what sorts of conceptual and procedural knowledge are important in these fields and how the affordances of graphic novels may provide opportunities to help technology and engineering teachers reach those goals. In addition, the Engineering chapter includes more research on comprehension and communication requirements in that field. But we are awaiting solid research about how graphic novels can help students learn and reach these goals.

Graphic Novels Are Useful for Teaching Mathematics

As with science, how graphic novels can support mathematics in reaching disciplinary goals is an area in need of further research. Some studies of how young adult literature can help bridge students' interest in mathematics touch on graphic novels but do not focus on them. Other studies about using graphic novels to teach STEM touch on mathematics, but do not focus on it. From what work has been done, however, we can begin to see where and how graphic novels could be helpful in teaching math.

Ho, Klanderman, Klanderman, and Turner (2023) discuss the use of a graphic novel to explore topics in geometry at the university level and report favorable attitudes from preservice teachers. While Siebert and Draper (2012) don't specifically address the use of graphic novels in the classroom, they do describe the ways that mathematicians use literacy, and how math teachers can apprentice their students to use literacy to reach instructional goals in the areas of computational fluency, conceptual understanding and mathematical processes (p. 177). Siebert and Draper go on to discuss how, provided we understand that numbers, symbols, and diagrams are part of literacy, a mathematics classroom is a literacy-rich environment, and a mathematics teacher can use language and texts to help students develop skills that are necessary for a fuller understanding of the discipline of mathematics. This work suggests that graphic novels can provide important ways to use literacy to reach disciplinary goals in math.

Koellner, Wallace, and Swackhamer (2009) considered how literature in general might best be used to support mathematics learning in middle school. They considered five content standards from the National Council for the Teaching of Mathematics (NCTM): numbers and operations, algebra, geometry, measurement, and data analysis and probability, as well as one NCTM process standard: problem-solving. They then looked at thirteen books aimed at middle school that connected with these standards. Unfortunately, they did not include any graphic novels in their list. They did find, however, that it was not difficult to find popular, high-interest literature that supported mathematics instruction across three levels of complexity.

Boerman-Cornell, Manderino, and Kim (2017) identify three habits of thinking associated with mathematics: justifying a mathematical claim, solving, and proving. They also identify three mathematical habits of practice: quantitative reasoning, communicating with precision, and persevering in problem-solving, again showing how graphic novels can be used to teach these habits.

While Darragh's (2018) content analysis of how young adult literature portrays mathematics in school seems to have overlooked graphic novels, it does address student perceptions of mathematics. Later we will argue that by bridging interests, graphic novels can help turn students' negative interests around. Darraugh's research showed that of the young adult fiction books considered, thirty-one out of fifty-nine novels contained references to mathematics instruction that positioned this instruction as negative. Seventeen of the novels positioned mathematics as neutral. The remaining books in the corpus positioned mathematics as positive (7) or were categorized as having a mixed portrayal (4). While it may not be true for all graphic novels, in reading graphic novels for this book, we certainly found many that skewed more positively in terms of their portrayal of math. Darragh's study is a good reminder that the stories about math that students are exposed to (whether in or out of school) have an effect on how they think about math and their own relation to it. While we cannot prevent students' exposure to negative portrayals, in books, other media, or social interactions, using well-chosen graphic novels as supplemental texts can at least provide a counter-narrative that offers a place for math in the student's life. This book will discuss these ideas further in the math chapter.

One other topic deserves discussion, the idea of using supplementary texts to bridge interest from one academic discipline to another (or from one area of interest to an academic discipline). A student interested in history, for example, might read a book that contains a topic that student is interested in (the development of the atomic bomb during the Second World War), and in reading that they might become interested in a topic from another academic discipline that connects to the topic that originally drew them in (the physics of the atomic bomb). A teacher may be able to fan the flame of that interest, and the end result is a student interested in multiple subjects (or at least not as negatively predisposed as they once were). For instance, one study on this topic by Boerman-Cornell, Klanderman, and Schut (2017) found that the *Harry Potter* series has the potential to bridge high-interest literature with higher dimensionality in mathematics.

And so, while there is a great deal of research that still needs to be done into how graphic novels can best support mathematics instruction, the research that is out there suggests some specific potential in reaching instructional goals in mathematics.

How to Get the Most Out of This Book

This book is organized to include chapters on science, technology, engineering, and mathematics, in that order. We understand and sympathize with the temptation to cherry-pick only the chapters that reflect what a particular reader teaches. Science teachers will gravitate toward the science chapters. Math teachers will skip to the math chapter, and so on. We would encourage you, however, to read beyond the chapters that seem to apply most directly to your teaching or interest. The reason that the STEM acronym exists at all is that the elements of STEM are so completely intertwined.

Engineering relies on the tools of math, technology, and science to design and build systems that change our lives. Science uses math for measurement and theory, technology for investigation and analysis, and engineering to build the tools necessary to investigate hypotheses. Technology relies on mathematics to code and encrypt, engineering to build microprocessors that make computing possible, and science to investigate, innovate, and test new developments like nanotechnology, AI, or countless other developments. Mathematics is more interesting to students (at least initially) if teachers can show applications to the fields of science, engineering, and technology. All the elements of STEM are connected.

And so, while we have separated these disciplines into their component chapters, there is a great deal of crossover. Further, graphic novels are often written across the STEM disciplines. For example, one graphic novel, *T-Minus* (2009), appears in chapters on all four disciplines. To learn the most about how to teach with graphic novels in the STEM classroom, we recommend reading all the chapters. For convenience, the Appendix is organized by discipline and includes comprehensive summaries of a variety of graphic novels. We also highlight many graphic novels on our website, gnclassroom.com, and continue to add to that collection as additional graphic novels are written.

In many of the chapters, readers will notice an organizational framework that references three general ways that graphic novels can be used in the classroom: to **Excite**, to **Explain**, and to **Enhance**. Graphic novels can increase student motivation to learn a particular topic by providing images, stories, or applications that excite them. Graphic novels can offer visualization and description of processes across time that can help explain concepts to students. And graphic novels can be used to enhance instruction, either by offering a chance for students who are struggling with a concept to see that idea from another perspective and to review it until it is clear—or for those students who are comprehending the learning of the class and are hungry for more by giving them further material to consider.

This chapter has presented research that argues that graphic novels may be a tool that can transform your teaching. We are confident that studies coming in the next few years will confirm what existing studies are finding, that graphic novels offer unique affordances for teaching across all the STEM fields. In the chapters that come, we will explore how a growing number of both nonfiction and fiction graphic novels that focus on science, technology, engineering, and math, can offer ways for teachers to effectively help reach disciplinary goals.

Art Notes

In planning this book, we considered extending to disciplines more broadly by including the arts in order to think of STEAM rather than STEM. We ultimately decided that the disciplinary goals in science, technology, engineering, and mathematics have a lot in common and that typically the disciplinary goals of art are different in such a way that including an art chapter would seem out-of-place and disconnected.

However, we recognize that not only are graphic novels literally composed of art, but that each of the disciplines of STEM is, and has always been, multimodal—that is to say, depending upon both words and text to make meaning. Science, for example, requires some form of artistic rendering to make models of processes understandable (consider the example at the beginning of this chapter). Technology, formerly built on a text-only interface, has moved through icons and images to click on to interfaces today that are very much visually dependent. Engineering uses drawn plans and blueprints (increasingly digital) in order to convey concepts, building instructions, and design elements to other experts and builders. Trying to do engineering without visual representation is almost unimaginable. And while geometry might come first to mind as a form of math that is highly image-dependent, higher-level math concepts, including, for example, dimensionality, are very much dependent on visual representations of models or applications.

And so, rather than a separate chapter for the arts, we will include, at the end of each chapter, a section called *Art Notes*, which will highlight the ways in which art and visual representation are tools that help us connect to disciplinary goals.

CHAPTER 2

Teaching Life Science and Earth Science with Graphic Novels

Consider three graphic novels:

In the Science Comics book titled *Volcanoes, Fire and Life* (2016), Jon Chad describes a future in which our ancestors are surviving in a new ice age by burning the remains of our world and using the books in a library to track and find the location of volcanoes that may be their only home. While the framing story is obviously fictional, the book itself does a great job of describing plate tectonics, causes of volcanoes, the types of rock that result from different volcanic conditions, different types of volcanoes, what causes eruptions, and more. This book uses graphic novel conventions to relate factual information and the concepts that connect those facts.

Darryl Cunningham's *Graphic Science: Seven Journeys of Discovery* (2017) uses spare drawings and extensive narration to tell the stories of Mary Anning, George Washington Carver, and Alfred Wegener, among others. The biographical sketches are short, and each focuses on what happens when a scientist's curiosity and drive to know bumps up against obstacles and difficulties.

Mary Anning discovered the fossilized remains of many dinosaurs and had a deep understanding of their classification and anatomy, though she was rarely credited by the scientists who used her as a guide and bought the fossils she found.

George Washington Carver was one of the first African Americans to earn a master's in agricultural science. He taught and researched at the Tuskegee Institute (eventually training Black farmers to use scientific farming to improve their yields and rotate crops), found a remarkable number of uses for peanuts, and popularized the crop both as restorative for the soil and a nutritious meal.

Alfred Wegener, a pioneer in meteorology, set records in ballooning, went on an Antarctic expedition, wrote a meteorology textbook, and eventually developed the theory that the continents had once been connected and that their movement had to do with continental drift. His theories and evidence were rejected because they went against the prevailing ideas of the time and because he was a meteorologist asserting a theory about geology, which was not his field. His ideas were confirmed thirty-five years later, after he had died.

Finally, the graphic novel *Primates: The Fearless Science of Jane Goodall, Dian Fossey, and Biruté Galdikas* (2013) by Jim Ottaviani and Maris Wicks tells the story of three women, all recruited by Louis Leakey, who used extensive, long-term, embedded observation to learn about the social systems of different groups of primates. The emphasis in this book is on the importance of detailed observation and recording as well as the idea of coming to a particular scientific puzzle without preconceptions. All three scientists had intense interests in their subjects and were recruited by Leakey because they did not have extensive expertise and the presumptions that go with it. Maris Wicks uses recurring visual motifs to lead the reader to consider parallels between the women.

These three books described above cover a range of approaches (fictional framing story, short thematically connected biographical sketches, and related biographies of three scientists studying similar material with similar methodologies). The three books have a range of types of information they are conveying (factual and conceptual data about volcanoes, historical data about important yet not well-known scientists, and biographical and inspirational information about three women who studied primates). And the three books might be used in different ways to teach different aspects of life science and earth science (for direct instructions and explanation about volcanoes and plate tectonics, to extend student knowledge about science and scientists, and to bridge student interest to science for female students who might think science is not for them).

When we consider reading graphic novels for natural science content, we need to start with the understanding that there is a huge range of graphic novels about science, and each one has a different emphasis. As a result, teachers need to consider what objectives they have for their class (explanation, exposition, inspiration, connection or something else), and reflect on which resources best fit those purposes. But before we explore how students can read graphic novels and achieve course objectives, we have to start by explaining *how* to read graphic novels at all.

How to Read a Graphic Novel Page

On its most basic level, reading a graphic novel is simple. You start at the upper left page, unless you are reading manga in which case you start from the upper right (the term *manga* refers to a graphic novels drawn in a particular style which originated in Asia). You read that page, both the words and the images, then you either move to the right, or, if the first panel stretches all the way across the page, you move down. When you get to the bottom right of the page, you turn to the next page. As you read, you pay special attention to (and distinguish between) text boxes, speech balloons, and thought balloons.

But understanding a graphic novel fully is much more complicated than that. Students need to know how to evaluate, consider, and connect the information they are reading to prior knowledge and other sources (including textbooks and class explanations). In fact, graphic novels demonstrate the best approaches to information design (like many well-designed web pages or computer applications). Consider a simple example of the meaningful sequence of a graphic novel in how panels are displayed; this mirrors standard layouts that students may be familiar with in other contexts like when browsing a newspaper (Figure 2.1).

In an oversimplified sense, there are three top common design layouts: the Z-Pattern, Zig Zag Pattern, and F-Pattern. Modern web pages often use a variant of the F-Pattern, displaying the most important information on the left-hand side, and guiding the reader's eye to the right to see breakdowns or secondary information in sequence. The other two layouts (Z-Pattern and Zig Zag Pattern) are used most commonly within graphic novels to help to guide readers through information in a logical format. This helps the reader to ground themselves in the most important information (e.g., the start of a story or plot line in the top left corner) and matches how the human brain naturally digests information (in a crude sense). As readers spend more time with graphic novels, they become more attuned to the patterns and rhythms of information design, and it becomes increasingly familiar to them, which carries through into other disciplines and applications as well.

Perhaps it would be easier to use an example (Figure 2.2).

This is a page from *Last Things*, by Marissa Moss. This graphic memoir details Moss's husband's diagnosis and struggles with Amyotrophic Lateral Sclerosis (ALS) and is an excellent supplemental text for an anatomy class to remind students that disease affects humans, loved ones, and families.

This page has three panels, and we start with the one in the upper left corner. It is a split panel showing a drawn image and the photograph it is based on. The drawn image is necessary to guide the reader through the

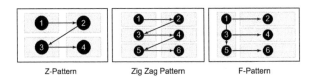

Z-Pattern   Zig Zag Pattern   F-Pattern

FIGURE 2.1 *Diagrams displaying common information design flows.*

143

FIGURE 2.2 *Example of the use of page layout and typography to convey information in* Last Things *(2017). Material used from* Last Things *© 2017, used with permission from Red Wheel/Weiser, LLC Newburyport, MA www.redwheelweiser.com.*

story (it might be hard for a reader to jump from a drawn image to a photo without the drawing. Readers might have trouble connecting the characters in the photo with the drawn characters on the previous page).

This panel has a text box at the top of the panel and another one at the bottom. Text boxes provide narration. Think of it as the third-person narrator in a book or a voice-over in a movie. Notice how, in order for the panel to make sense, we need to not only read the words and see the images, but we also have to connect the two. The words in the upper text box read

"He looks like he is staring at death while he clings to his sons' lives." Upon reading those words, the reader would then look at the images on the page to connect the comment with the image. Similarly, the lower text box is an observation by the narrator about the hollowness in Harvey's eyes. Again, the reader would look at the image. Interestingly, the photo doesn't show us Harvey's eyes, but we can see them in Moss's drawing. This might remind the reader that the narrator is drawing from her memories of the event in addition to the photo.

From the first panel, we move right to the second panel. This panel has text boxes like the last one, but it also has word balloons. The balloon on the right is the first one you read and, usually in a graphic novel, that means that the speech contained within that balloon comes first chronologically. When reading speech balloons in graphic novels that the writer/illustrator has hand-lettered, notice how the lettering sometimes conveys an emotion or a particular characteristic of the voice speaking. In this case, Harvey's lettering is shaky and wanders up and down in the balloon. When we read his voice then, we need to think of it as shaky, perhaps whispery and unsteady.

The reader then looks to the next panel, which takes up the lower half of the page. Here too, there are text boxes and word balloons, but the focus of the panel is Harvey with his shirt off. We are clearly meant to have a strong reaction to how thin his body is, especially in relation to the topic of the conversation, how he needs more calories and is losing weight.

The other thing to remember about reading graphic novels is that the eye must often dart back and forth between panels to see what things have changed as time passes. For example, in panel two, we can see that Marissa's facial expression looks like a smile. This makes sense in light of the bottom text box which conveys a hint of hope. In contrast, her expression in the third panel is one of worry. To really understand graphic novels, the reader needs to always be reading not only the panel they are focused on but also the panel that came before and the one that will follow.

It is important to remember that this explanation slows the reading process down. When an experienced graphic novel reader is looking at a page, much of this process happens all at once. Perhaps the best way to instruct students to read graphic novels is to project a page from a graphic novel onto a whiteboard and ask them how they read it and what they notice as they read. Some university teachers have used this exercise in class and in teacher in-services and affirm how students (and teachers) pick up on new things every time this exercise is conducted that they may have missed, even when they have read the same passage themselves multiple times.

Knowing how to read a graphic novel generally is useful. But the focus of this chapter is using graphic novels to help students learn to read *science*. For that we need to take a look at how students might best read scientifically.

Learning Science

Before we can describe how graphic novels can be used as effective tools to teach the natural sciences, we need to be clear about some of the foundational concepts and structures students need to know to think like a scientist. These structures and concepts are present to some extent in every science unit any student learns from kindergarten through grad school.

Boerman-Cornell, Manderino, and Kim (2017) argue that students need to understand that to know something in science is to understand that the field " . . . is constantly expanding and all constructs and theories are challenged and tested" (p. 10). The skills that students need to learn to think like a scientist are "Questioning, hypothesizing, and model building" (p. 10). Further, students need to learn how to construct models of scientific processes, write explanations of those processes, and read visual representations of scientific concepts, processes, and structures (p. 10).

This means that science should not be taught as static knowledge to be memorized. Similarly, the scientific method should not be taught as a procedure which, if followed, will result in predictable results (although that can be true in some classroom exercises), but as a method of inquiry that leads to the discovery of new knowledge. And students should be taught that science is more than accurately gathering data (though it includes that), but is also about building a model to explain how that data reflects a process.

Bransford and Donovan (2005) suggest that students need to learn to address preconceptions (p. 399), understand what it means to do science (p. 403), and how to think about their own thinking processes (metacognition) (p. 407).

Their argument is that before students can learn to question existing science or engage their curiosity fully, they need to think about what preexisting explanations they subscribe to regarding phenomena and whether those assumptions are accurate. For example, many people believe that turning on a fan in a room with no windows cools down the room. Students must consider what idea this is based on. Does air get cooler when it moves around? How does sweat cool people? Do electric motors generate heat as a byproduct? How much heat do humans emit from their bodies? After thinking about these things, can it be true that a fan cools down the air? Once students have addressed their preconceptions, they can begin working on conceptual change. Would it be more accurate to think of the fan moving cool air into a room if a window is open (and it is cooler outside than inside)? Could it be that a fan in a closed room seems to cool down the air because the air moving across us is causing our sweat to evaporate, which cools us down?

Understanding what it means to do science is understanding that science is not memorizing facts (though doing so may help a scientist do their job), but rather learning content by " . . . actively engaging in processes of scientific inquiry" (Bransford & Donovan, 2005, p. 405). This means students need to learn how to imagine interactions on both a macro and micro level (including some interactions that they cannot see visually), how to generate hypotheses, and to experience the excitement of learning about something that no one else on the planet understands yet.

Real science involves thinking about the way one thinks and questioning that critically. This reasoning involves asking ourselves how we know what we know, what unseen processes we imagine cause things to happen the way they do, and if there are other ways we could think about those things. Students should learn to fight the stubborn tendency we have to rely on the way we understand things or the way we are told that things happen. Learning to assemble data in other ways to reach different conclusions can be helpful. Of course, this metacognitive thinking needs to be ultimately rooted in factual understanding.

Minstrell and Kraus (2005) argue that if we want to teach our students these concepts and ways of practice, we need to approach teaching differently. In order for students to be able to change their preconceptions, teachers need to start by asking students what they are thinking, and then listening " . . . respectfully to what they say" (p. 464). Next, we need to understand that "Learning is an active process" (p. 476) and because of that we need to " . . . acknowledge students' attempts to make sense of their experiences and help them confront inconsistencies . . . " (p. 464) in what they are thinking. In questioning them, we need to try to ask the sorts of questions that students might ask themselves as they are trying to figure out a preconception, concept, or structure.

While it is true that science teachers need to help students learn to apply the scientific method to their thinking, they also need to help students question their presuppositions, use imagination to think metacognitively about different ways to assemble data into mental models of what might be going on with a particular process, and consider multiple hypotheses and test them mentally against a model as well as physically with data. And teachers need to do this by opening up the classroom with questioning and listening that gives students the opportunity to do all that without fear of a line of reasoning turning out to be wrong. As we shall see later in the chapter, there are some ways graphic novels can help with that. But first we need to consider how graphic novels relate to science literacy.

Reading Science

Shanahan (2012) points out that reading in science does not involve one single set of skills for all branches. Chemists, for example, use knowledge of chemical structures and experimentation to see the effects of what is often happening on an unseen atomic level. Some biologists and ecologists might rely on direct observation of nature, looking for interesting phenomena (p.154). Other biologists might be looking for answers about the same animals, but by considering their genetic make-up (p. 155). Not surprisingly, the way the different branches of science select, evaluate, and use information from texts also varies.

Science textbooks do not often take this into account. Shanahan (2012) points out that science textbooks are dense with vocabulary. In fact, according to some researchers, science textbooks are more dense than any other type of textbook. When students are not taught how to understand the structure of a textbook or how and what to pay attention to, they often have great difficulty determining which information is relevant, or reading it conceptually rather than just for facts.

Shanahan points out that sometimes science teachers, in an attempt to help their struggling students, do not hold students accountable for what they have read and instead explain it orally. On the one hand, it could be argued that this is good modeling for students to make sense of what the textbook says. The unintended result, however, is that students stop engaging with the text at all and wait for the oral explanation. It also means that instead of trying to make sense of the textbook on their own, they are writing down what the teacher says without necessarily considering it for themselves. Instead of teaching students to learn how to understand and participate in scientific discourse, teachers end up training students to take notes. And, as a consequence, labs and lab reports, while valuable, become disconnected from the concepts being taught in the textbook (p. 155).

Shanahan cites studies that have argued that the problem with this approach is that science texts have great potential for helping students consider and re-evaluate their presuppositions. Further, when students do experiments without engaging in the conceptual understanding, they can actually reinforce their mistaken preconceived notions. Shanahan describes an example of an experiment in which students developed different types of packaging to enable them to drop eggs out of a third-story window to determine whether the eggs would fall at the same speed with different packaging. After dropping the eggs and doing the measurements, most of the students were so convinced that heavier objects fall faster that when the data did not bear that out, they concluded that something was wrong with the experiment (p. 157).

After considering this and similar research, Shanahan concludes that students (and perhaps some teachers) read science texts differently than scientists do. In a study conducted in 2008, Shanahan interviewed chemists about what and how they read, then contrasted that with other interviews of other experts. She found that vocabulary in science can be difficult because many terms have both a general meaning and several specific scientific meanings. She gives an example of the word *evaporate*, which in the general world often has a meaning synonymous with disappearing. In chemistry, however, it refers specifically to matter changing from a liquid to a gaseous state (p. 159–60). Shanahan also found that the scientists she interviewed read the text looking for concepts rather than facts (which is how many students read a text). Many students (as was mentioned earlier in Chapter 1 of this book) read the primary textual flow, but skip right over graphs, illustrations, and tables. Shanahan's overall conclusion is that teachers do not merely need to teach students to read, they need to teach them to read science in the ways that scientists read. Fortunately, as we shall see shortly, graphic novels can help.

How Can Graphic Novels Help Students Question Their Suppositions?

Regular textbooks have a powerful tool at their disposal when confronting inaccurate presuppositions, and that is the authority of print. When students see dark print in a Times New Roman or other authoritative font, they tend to accept what is printed there as true. However, most science teachers would argue that it is more helpful if students confront their mistaken assumptions logically and critically, go through cognitive dissonance, and resolve the contradiction in their mind with a new, correct understanding of the concept. Being overruled by an authoritative textbook may not engender the kind of comprehension and conviction that will help students. And the bottom line is, authoritative print sometimes struggles to overcome perceived experience. If a student reads in a textbook that a bowling ball falls at the same speed as a tennis ball, but they have had the experience of dropping a bowling ball on their foot, they may perceive, because the bowling ball hurt so much, that it was falling faster. That is because they have seen (and in this case felt) a bowling ball fall, and it seems to the student that the ball fell very fast. A graphic novel can use both the authority of print and the experiential feeling of seeing an image to fight against misperception.

For example, Andy Hirsch's *Science Comics: Cats: Nature and Nurture* (2019) addresses the mistaken presupposition that there are cougars (also called mountain lions, pumas, and several other names) that are melanistic (possessing a dark-colored coat of fur). While there have been thousands of alleged sightings of "black panthers" across the United States, no black panther has ever been proven to exist (via photograph, carcass, or any other evidence). Page 24 of Hirsch's book addresses this in five panels, which we will describe in detail here.

The first panel features two text boxes at the top that describe this misperception, that many people think they have seen a black panther in the United States but the only big cat native to the United States is the cougar, which is never darkly colored. So how is this possible? The panel then has an illustration of an animal control officer talking on the phone while affixing a pin to a map of the United States. A word balloon captures his conversation in which he is sarcastically repeating what the person is telling him, that there is a black panther and it is stuck in their tree and then he asks how big the cat is. We know his words are sarcastic because we can see his facial expression with heavily lidded eyes and an utter lack of concern or interest.

The second panel is smaller and shows the woman calling the animal control officer. She is inside a house and just outside her window is what appears to be a housecat in a tree, but because it is dark and the cat is backlit, it appears to be all black and a bit larger than its actual size. A text box explains that a lot of the reported animal settings are likely large domesticated cats in trees.

The third panel shows a panicked camper talking into his phone (perhaps he is the one talking to animal control). It is night time and he is pointing to a hill or ridge upon which a big cat is silhouetted by the moon. The text box explains that the sighting might be of an ordinary brown cougar in deep shadow.

The fourth panel suggests that sometimes the sighting might be all in the imagination of the person who is reporting it. The illustration shows a frightened person all but hiding under their covers and the light from a night light shining on a cat alarm clock throwing a scary shadow on the wall.

The final panel on the page features the house cat that has been narrating the story throughout the book addressing the readers and explaining that if black cougars do exist, they must be phenomenally good at hiding.

This page combines clear authoritative text explaining that no black panthers have ever been seen, while the images allow the reader to see how it is possible that people think they are seeing a melanistic big cat when they aren't. The page also uses humor to position the reader as someone who is in on the joke, seeing the ways that people are being fooled into making a mistaken sighting and sympathizing with the animal control officer who has heard it all before.

While there is not necessarily a science graphic novel for every mistaken assumption that students might have, exposing students to graphic novels that debunk mistaken conclusions could help students begin to think in ways that will help them question their presuppositions. Darryl Cunningham's *How to Fake a Moon Landing* (2013) is a good example of a book that debunks false presuppositions as well as conspiracy theories that question the veracity of science. This graphic novel includes controversial topics such as homeopathy, the MMR vaccination scandal, evolution, and climate change, all put under the critical lens of science. However, many other graphic novels have similar moments of questioning presuppositions. To guide such discussions of potential cognitive dissonance, teachers can use a projector to take the entire class through short excerpts that address mistaken presuppositions.

How Can Graphic Novels Encourage Imagination and Metacognitive Thinking?

Sometimes we position science as caring only about facts and data. And while data certainly forms the backbone of science, imagination is a vital component as well. Once we have gathered the data, we need to consider what that data means, how it works, and how it fits together. To build a model of how that data interacts often requires a leap, however.

Consider Copernicus, who had to reject the presupposition of his day (and throughout much of history before as well) that the Earth was what the rest of the universe rotated around. Using the same data many astronomers before him had, Copernicus postulated a universe in which the sun was the center, and the Earth and other planets orbited around it. This required him to imagine a model that would fit the observations of the stars and planets that he and others had made.

Or consider German chemist August Kekule, who in 1865, allegedly with the help of a dream in which he saw a snake gripping its tail in its mouth, was able to imagine the structure of the benzene molecule as a hexagonal ring of carbon atoms.

How can graphic novels help students learn to exercise their imagination in scientific thinking? There are two ways that graphic novels can do this. First is by modeling the thinking processes of influential scientists through graphic novel biographies, such as those of biologists Jane Goodall, Dian Fossey, Biruté Galdikas (Ottaviani & Wicks 2013), fossil discoverer Mary Anning, botanist George Washington Carver (Cunningham 2017), naturalist Edward O. Wilson (Wilson, Ottaviani, & Butzer, 2020), and others.

These graphic novels effectively tell the stories of moments when scientists use their imaginations to develop a new conclusion or new way of seeing with the data that they have. This sort of modeling can show students what the best scientists do.

The second way might seem like more of a stretch, but we would argue that it is not. When students first learn to read, in early elementary school, teachers frequently read books out loud to students. This requires the students to listen to the words and practice imagining the settings, characters, and actions in their minds. This seeing-in-the-mind is the main component of imagination. It is also a time when nearly every student enjoys reading.

Somewhere around fourth grade, read-alouds become far less common and students transition from reading for fun to reading to learn. They suddenly must master reading in all the academic subjects, and many of the supports (including read-alouds) disappear. This increase of demand and decrease of support and motivation often also results in a decrease of enjoying reading as well as a decrease in practicing imagination.

Scott McCloud first suggested in the book *Understanding Comics* (1994) that the gutter, the space between two panels, is the center of imagination in a graphic novel or comic book. McCloud contends that as the reader transitions from one visual panel to the next, the reader must imagine the action that happens between those two panels. So, if the first panel shows a character running up the sidewalk to a house, and the second panel shows the character bursting into the living room and yelling something about a dragon on the loose, the reader has to imagine how the character got from the walk to the living room. They must imagine the character opening the door and running down the hallway into the living room. That act of imagination happens multiple times on each page of a graphic novel. We contend that it is likely that the mere act of reading graphic novels sharpens the imagination. To be sure, this improved micro-imagination is not the same as the leap of imagination required to reconceptualize a structure or system based on data, but we believe that graphic novels scaffold the seeing-in-the-mind nature of imagination and that honing those skills are important to really do science.

It is also true that graphic novels can help students visualize things that cannot be seen. Graphic novels can show the insides of volcanoes in cross section, the progression of mitosis, the activity inside of a dark hive of honey bees, the life cycle of sharks, the orbits of comets, and many other things that are difficult or impossible to photograph. What's more, graphic novels can use multiple panels to help students visualize growth, progression, and change in those situations. And once students get used to visualizing things that they cannot see, when it is time for them to make sense of anomalous data, conceptualize a new idea, or imagine what it is like on a cellular level for a wound to heal, they will be better prepared to do so.

How do Graphic Novels Help Students Learn Vocabulary?

While we do not have time nor space for a full discussion of the research that looks at teaching vocabulary, there are several fully researched and widely accepted understandings about how best to help students learn vocabulary. We will distill that research down to three general principles:

1. Vocabulary is best learned in context. While having students memorize definitions and respond on an assessment to show that they have memorized those definitions seems like a good practice (and certainly gives the teacher the illusion of control), students do not necessarily apply these terms technically as intended. When students learn by definition, assessments reveal that while they might have a strong receptive vocabulary—which

is to say that they can often recognize the word when they are reading and understand the sense of it in that sentence—words learned solely by memorization do not as readily enter their active vocabulary. That means that students are not able to use that word correctly or consistently appropriately in their own speaking and writing.

If students instead learn to determine the meaning of a word by reading it in context and looking at how it is used in a sentence and how the structure and content of that sentence gives them clues as to the meaning of the word, students are not only more likely to have the word enter their active vocabulary, but they will be more able to add new words to their vocabulary independently of their teacher's instruction and at a faster rate.

2. Effectively learning vocabulary in context ideally requires that the student encounter the word more than once, or in multiple and varied contexts. Walter Kintsch (1988, 1998) suggested that when we read, we are constantly building and taking down a series of propositional ideas or statements. So, when experienced readers encounter a new word, they make up their best guess as to its meaning based on the context in which it appears and then read on. If the word appears again in another sentence, the reader is able to refine their mental provisional definition and modify their understanding. For each new context the reader encounters the word in, they gain a fuller understanding of the meaning of the word and how to apply it.

3. Building off these two understandings, one of the most accepted ways to teach vocabulary through direct instruction is to divide a piece of paper (or blank document) into four (or sometimes six) boxes. In one box, the student writes the definition. In a second box, they used the word in a sentence. In a third box, they draw a picture of the word. In the fourth box, they write examples of the word, or its essential and non-essential characteristics, or some variation thereof. This approach is sometimes referred to as the Frayer Model.

All three of these understandings are supported by the format of graphic novels. When an unfamiliar word is introduced to readers in a graphic novel, it, of course, has the textual context of the sentence it is being used in. Additionally, it has the context of the full expression of the character uttering the word and whatever is happening in the image. It may also have the context of the ways in which the text is interacting with the images. Consider this example from Jay Hosler's *The Way of the Hive* (Figure 2.3).

FIGURE 2.3 *The use of text and image interplay to enrich information and hold the reader's attention in* The Way of the Hive (2021, p. 12-13).

The biological concept and term being communicated here (and of course, this is an excerpt, removed from the context of the rest of the book) is not simple, but unlike a lecture, here when we learn about metamorphosis, the reader can back up, reread Hosler's words, and reconsider the images until the concept makes sense. Further, Hosler renders in detail the differences between the two stages of a honeybee's development, while emphasizing that the two forms are the same creature (notice the second panel at the top of the second page of this spread, in which the adult bee and the larva share a split screen image, with half of each face being shown). Hosler is able to use a narrative story to hold reader's attention while embedding important information in the storyline (consider the upper right-hand corner of the spread, and notice how easily this information fits in the story).

In other parts of the same graphic novel, Hosler can show readers cutaways of the comb, diagram the movements bees use to communicate location and distance to food sources and show us the inside of a beehive in ways that readers can make sense of, when a photo might be too crowded and static for readers to decipher. If Hosler, an expert bee researcher and gifted artist, can envision it, he can depict it in a way that invites readers to imagine it too.

How Graphic Novels Help Student Readers Consider Data and Diagrams

Earlier in this chapter we talked about how, in conventional science textbooks, there is usually a primary textual flow—the main text that students read. That primary textual flow is often broken up by graphs, photographs, charts, and illustrations. The authors of the textbooks and the science teachers alike hope that students are engaging with the textual flow and the charts and images. In fact, Shanahan and others have pointed out that when scientists read journal articles, they read the primary textual flow, look at the chart or data, and look back at the primary textual flow, often alternating between the two several times as they seek to understand the connections between the two. Unfortunately, student readers often privilege the text over the charts, data, and illustrations.

Graphic novels not only make it much harder to ignore the ancillary charts and data by embedding them in the panel progressions in each page, but they also model the way students should read a science text with charts, data, or illustrations.

Having explored ways in which graphic novels can benefit students who are learning and reading science in general, we can now turn to the natural sciences more specifically. Because of the diversity of the natural sciences, we will focus first on life and earth science in this chapter and then physical sciences in the next.

Life Sciences

Teachers in the life sciences face distinct and unique challenges that are different from their physical sciences counterparts. Life sciences courses are sometimes perceived as having a lower mathematical requirement, and therefore as being easier to succeed in for students who do not see themselves as successful in science. As such, life sciences teachers often face the daunting task of teaching and fostering the fundamental elements of science literacy, and an upward battle of convincing students who may be focused on more applied career paths (e.g., doctors, nurses) that topics like ecology and microbiology are relevant and important. Life sciences teachers also may need to work harder to connect concepts like experimental design to important aspects of more focused applications.

Like physical sciences teachers, life sciences teachers also must contend with concepts that need to be seen on micro and macro levels at the same time. Understanding human biology, for example, requires an understanding of molecular biology, what is happening on a bacterial level in the gut, how larger muscle groups and organs function, and how large populations respond to generational and environmental changes over large geographic spaces and millions of years of time.

Graphic novels can help students be better equipped with an understanding of fundamental micro and macro concepts and have a closer understanding of the connection between concepts and skills developed in class and applications in the professional and scientific research world. Later we discuss case studies of how graphic novels can be applied to deepen student engagement and knowledge retention for future applications. We will consider how graphic novels can serve as a gateway to science literacy, how they can tie foundational learning into the scientific method, and increase accessibility to a diverse set of problems.

Graphic Novels to Explain: Life Sciences as the Gateway to Science Literacy

Arching over the entirety of science education is the preparation of students to filter and respond to the vast amount of scientific information produced in today's society. From the US 2015 National Science Assessment, 22 percent of twelfth-grade students tested at proficient or above; with no progress since 2009 (National Center for Education Statistics, 2015). The students who need science literacy the most may be those who are not intending to follow a science-based career. And as we said earlier in the chapter, most textbooks do not make this task any easier. In addition to the flood of knowledge they are responsible to convey, textbooks also need to present ideas that are still in development—concepts that scientists have not yet reached a consensus on. In general, this presents an ocean of material for students to learn, which is particularly hard if they have not yet mastered science vocabulary and foundational concepts. This, in turn, only widens the gap between those who can look at a large table of data, for example, and understand and interpret results and those who are struggling to know what to look at and how to look at it.

Graphic novels can engage students, apprentice them into the language and conceptual vocabulary of science, and help them process and remember content, making it easier to understand the ideas being taught. The interweaving of pictures and text in the graphic novel format gives students multiple contexts for understanding and helps to drive enjoyment and excitement in science where it might not already exist. For example, integrating a graphic novel like *How to Fake a Moon Landing: Exposing the Myths of Science Denial* (Cunningham & Revkin, 2013) brings a conversational style to addressing heavy topics like climate change denial and issues like the MMR vaccine autism trials and homeopathy. Using the structures introduced in the book, teachers can lead students through *Mythbusters*-style projects where they challenge and either confirm or reject current summaries of scientific studies, misinformation available on the internet, conspiracy theories, and utterly odd assertions (like the assertion that the Earth is flat, or the statement that a high school teacher friend of ours reported recently—that Helen Keller's blindness was a hoax). Addressing the veracity of claims that purport to be scientific or logical builds student skills and intuition for future science literacy and understanding.

This work is particularly important in life sciences to ensure students who are intimidated by more mathematically intensive fields like the physical sciences still develop crucial core science literacy skills to create a well-informed generation able to challenge and filter misinformation and misconceptions as insight-driven decisions backed by science become the norm.

In addition to topics that serve as gateways, consider the common topics covered in books like Maris Wicks's *Human Body Theater* (2015). While pitched to middle school and upper elementary readers, the book offers a remarkably comprehensive and accurate set of explanations of the skeletal, muscular, respiratory, cardiovascular, digestive, excretory, endocrine, reproductive, immune, and nervous systems with a final section on the senses. The book features a skeleton who guides the reader through the body's systems, organs that explain themselves, and a good amount of humor throughout. The style is conversational and doesn't shy away from pointing out how amazing the body is. In short, it is a book that reads more like a course taught by an engaging teacher than a forced slog through a textbook and would be an excellent companion to a human anatomy textbook.

Similarly, *Science Comics: Coral Reefs: Cities of the Ocean* (2016) also by Wicks, defines what a coral reef is, how they are formed and where they are, the ecosystem that lives in and around coral reefs, (including everything from flatworms to giant clams), how the ecosystems of coral reefs are connected to the rest of the planet, and challenges and changes affecting the coral reefs of the world. Any course or unit focusing on ecosystems and the interconnectedness of all life on the planet could use this book as a jumping-off point. Such graphic novels can also serve as a great conversation starter for issues related to the environment and the impact of humanity on other species.

Regardless of whether students pursue a career in life sciences or otherwise, a foundational understanding of things that affect their day-to-day life, like the human body or the environment, will pay dividends in equipping them as citizens. Oftentimes, foundational knowledge like nutrition, physical fitness, or climate change is wrapped in the umbrella of "science" which many students immediately tune out of, to their own long-term detriment. Graphic novel examples like the ones mentioned here can help with jarring students out of their daily mindsets of tuning out science class and instead thinking of science as something worthwhile to pay attention to. Maybe, just maybe, a graphic novel may be able to get a student to admit that the human body is an amazing machine or transport them to mentally encounter coral reefs they may never get the opportunity to touch themselves.

Graphic Novels to Enhance: Tying Foundational Learning into the Scientific Method

One of the biggest challenges as a life sciences teacher is to connect the foundational work and understanding necessitated within the curriculum to the overarching application of the scientific method. Life sciences can often feel disjointed to students in the sheer amount of base knowledge necessary for proficiency. Students in a life sciences course spend large amounts of time memorizing facts, definitions, and other foundational knowledge in order to apply it within the proper context and can often get lost in actually applying it using a hypothesis-driven experimental framework.

The story mapping of a graphic novel inherently lends itself to the development of key life sciences concepts, including the full scientific and exploratory context. Take for example *Stuff of Life* (Schultz, Cannon, & Cannon, 2009), the graphic novel detailing the complex processes and structures of DNA that we mentioned in Chapter 1. Not only does the book summarize the key concepts of DNA coding, roles of RNA, and their effects on human traits, it prefaces all of these learnings at the beginning of each chapter with "DNA from a Human Perspective," outlining the key figures, hypotheses, and experiments that took place as a part of the modern understanding of DNA. Integrating a book like this as a chronological guide within a DNA unit can help students not only better understand the fundamental interactions necessary for DNA and genes, but also how scientists affirmed or rejected hypotheses in order to produce those results. Students can continually reinforce their understanding of what good science looks like in the context of each of their units like DNA to prepare them for independent scientific approaches in the future.

Primates: The Fearless Science of Jane Goodall, Dian Fossey, and Biruté Galdikas (2013) by Jim Ottaviani and illustrated by Maris Wicks describes a more long-form scientific method where three scientists commissioned by Louis Leakey did amazing naturalistic observational studies of the communities and habits of three different species of primates. This book could be helpful to make the distinction between experimentation and analysis and naturalistic observational studies, as well as being inspirational, particularly for women interested in going into science. This graphic novel could supplement a class text, could be handed to students who might enjoy supplemental reading, could be used as a remedial aid for students who need to read another explanation to help them grasp what a textbook is getting at, and could be used as a classroom library book for anyone who might be interested in this specific topic.

Another way to enhance students' learning experience is to connect back to the real world. Marissa Moss's *Last Things* (2017), mentioned earlier in this chapter, is a memoir of caring for and eventually having to say goodbye to a husband with ALS, or Lou Gehrig's disease. While the medical references in this book are solid, its real value lies in helping human anatomy or physiology students realize the human cost of disease, perhaps also serving as a motivation for students considering a career in medical science. Any unit focused on pathology or the nervous system would be enhanced with a book like this. In a similar vein, we can bring new life and contexts to topics that are often merely given lip service, like indigenous knowledge in the scientific context.

Let's pause a moment and unpack the concept of indigenous knowledge. While not all of you reading are treaty people of Turtle Island (North America), there are distinct people groups on the various continents around the world who discovered and understood many of the concepts that took settlers years to understand as a result of living in close harmony with nature. One shortcoming of modern science is often to discount or discard this knowledge in favor of things that are more comfortable or familiar, like scientific papers or structured environmental studies. As settlers conversed with indigenous cultures, they often heard stories of gods or spirits that would drive natural phenomena, like the prevalence of the raven in Haida mythology on the west coast of Canada who released the sun resulting in the creation of the stars and the moon. To date, often this seems like a far-fetched notion, especially as people would propose trying to use these stories in order to form a basis for scientific knowledge or inquiry, which follows a robust structure, processes, and review.

As an example, consider Michael Yahgulanaas's *Carpe Fin* (2019). The story follows a man stranded on an island feeling the effects of a fuel spill. As Carpe encounters "the Lord of the Rock," this can feel like mysticism to some, and devoid of any connection to the scientific context. However, presenting this in the graphic novel context, a teacher can explore what truths are seen in the interaction between Carpe and the Lord of the Rock—what does Carpe know about the effects of the spill that can be translated or matched to the knowledge brought by a scientific study? Furthermore, what knowledge in our lives may be easily dismissed due to how it is communicated, thereby dismissing the value of the content? To this day, there are indigenous communities around the world with a closer understanding and connection to nature than many top scientists, yet they are often ignored or not consulted during studies that are highly related to their current or traditional ways of life. Graphic novels are an exceptional way to pause and reflect on this, especially since the knowledge is being portrayed in a way contrasting the traditional format (e.g., a scientific paper or textbook). As indigenous knowledge is often verbal, or remembered using stories, so can graphic novels use their interplay of stories, graphics, and knowledge to cement complex knowledge into our understanding.

As the example of *Carpe Fin* illustrates, graphic novels can enhance key overarching concepts for the classroom and the core values that science education needs to equip students.

Graphic Novels to Excite: Increasing Accessibility to Diverse Problems

It can be exciting for students to see connections across academic disciplines. Cross-disciplinary connections can also be a powerful tool for teachers to help students to bridge interest from one aspect of their lives to science. For example, a student who is wholly focused on a future career as a firefighter might be quick to dismiss math, science, English, and history as being irrelevant to that occupation. But if a science teacher connects that student with a graphic novel or other trade book about how fire investigators use the scientific method, mathematical formulas, and both the physical and life sciences to determine the origin and cause of a fire, that student's interest might be bridged to both science and math. Similarly, a student who may be passionate about the latest race cars or motorcycles may start appreciating thermodynamics if they can see the link to internal combustion engines in a book like *Science Comics: Cars* (Zettwoch, 2019).

Life sciences provide an immense diversity of opportunities to connect with other disciplines both in and out of school. Doing so helps students break out of narrow perspectives on data. For example, when students consider a career in life science they sometimes limit themselves to thinking about traditional occupations like nurses, physicians, or environmental scientists. However, in the increasingly cross-disciplinary world evolving from applications of technology and the need for deep subject matter expertise across disciplines, there are in fact far more opportunities for bridging expertise in the work world as well. Effective science communicators are needed not just in traditional scientist roles but also as science journalists, managers who can connect scientists with product designers and advertisers, science podcast producers, creators of science graphic novels, and so on.

Graphic novels can help to enrich this discovery through approachable, trusted information on topics that may not be considered by students initially. In-depth studies, like First Second's *Science Comics* series that dive into fields like the study of crows, bats, meteorology, sharks, the brain, dogs, cats, polar bears, volcanoes, the solar system, the chemistry of baking, robots, drones, skyscrapers, and trees, could introduce a fascinating field to a student who may not know the possible opportunities or exciting questions that are available to unpack.

We can also return to Jay Hosler's *The Way of the Hive* (originally published as *Clan Apis* back in 1998 and recently re-released by HarperCollins), which tells the story of Nyuki, a honeybee larva who is mentored by an older bee, Dvorah. We see Nyuki go through metamorphosis, learn how to cap cells, interpret the dances of other bees to seek out pollen, and eventually mourn the passing of his mentor, become a mentor himself, and eventually die. The story is remarkably moving, yet also conveys far more information than any textbook other than perhaps a graduate textbook on etymology would, but in a deeply engaging way. Hosler did his Ph.D. work specifically on bees and it shows. For many students, something seemingly as niche as studying bees as a full-time job may be illuminating, and this book could be a great way to teach everything from life cycles to adaptability and animal behavior.

Before we close the discussion of the life sciences, we would be remiss if we did not directly address one of the largest fields motivating students to pursue life sciences: medicine. Many students encounter or pursue careers in medicine because of witnessing over-dramatized television or the ten-minute interactions with their family doctor or a nurse in an emergency room. Graphic novels can help to paint a broader picture of what medicine can be by highlighting real, more subdued stories of what medicine looks like. As a byproduct of this, graphic novels can tell intimate stories at a surprising depth, which helps with the learning process of things like bedside manner.

We consider two contrasting examples of this: *Pedro and Me* (Winick 2000), a graphic novel about an intimate HIV/AIDS story, and *Fred & Marjorie* (Kerbel 2021), the story of the discovery of insulin. Both of these novels show very different aspects of medicine that a documentary, a textbook, or a traditional novel may miss. *Pedro and Me* touches on the heart-wrenching journey of a friend watching a twenty-two-year-old man die of HIV/AIDS, which can quickly build (or rebuild) the empathy necessary to be an effective medical practitioner. Contrasting this, *Fred & Marjorie* tells the story of a research doctor in Ontario, Canada, who underwent the taxing process of testing insulin in a laboratory setting and ultimately testing it and saving his first diabetic patient in 1922. Graphic novels like this not only highlight the scientific process that can go into drug discovery but also the ripple effects that the inventions can have—with insulin having such an incredible impact on the lives of millions today. Graphic novels related to medicine include some very detailed fiction as well, such as the *Graphic Medicine Manifesto* (Czerwiec et al., 2015). While we've touched on many of the same themes and topics here, the *Graphic Medicine Manifesto* delivers a first-hand account of medical school educators applying comics and graphic novels in situations like fourth-year seminar courses.

While we are not recommending replacing textbooks with graphic novels, graphic novels are a good way to achieve a particular science-specific goal, teaching students to interpret data from charts and connect it to larger concepts. This chapter has shown some ways graphic novels can do that for earth and life sciences. To that end, we recommend keeping some high-interest, science-based books in your classroom library for supplemental reading that may inspire and motivate students (see the Appendix or our website, gnclassroom.com, for titles). We also recommend using some graphic novels as remediation—an easy way to help students struggling with a specific concept to be able to review and understand at their own pace. Additionally, some graphic novels are excellent as supplementary texts, helping higher achievers (or the whole class) learn about particular subjects in more depth.

Our goal in this book is to show teachers ways in which graphic novels can help them reach specific goals they have for their students through supplementary use of graphic novels. This chapter, along with Chapter 1, provides the essentials necessary to understand the more in-depth chapters for each part of STEM learning. In addition to the next chapter about teaching physical science, we encourage science teachers to also read the technology, engineering, and math chapters as well, since STEM principles often extend beyond academic disciplinary boundaries.

Art Notes

We mentioned that graphic novels can use the authority of print and the experiential feeling of seeing an image in order to fight against misperceptions. There are, of course, other aspects of art that contribute to the unraveling of misperceptions. Art teachers might wish to point them out to their students.

One of the most distinctive aspects of the graphic novel medium is the way that the panels allow us to control the speed at which the reader moves through time. Panels allow graphic novel artists to make multiple drawings of a single subject, showing change to whatever degree of detail they wish. In doing so, graphic novel artists can illustrate scientific processes like evaporation, progressions like the development and movement of sedimentary rock, growth of plants or creatures, and cause and effect.

It is also worth noting that when we argued that graphic novels sharpen imagination and seeing-in-the-mind, we might also have pointed out that these are skills that contribute not only to developing scientific models, but also to the visualizing necessary within the mind even before brush, pen, or pencil touches paper for the artist. Once again we see that art education and learning science are not incompatible.

CHAPTER 3

Teaching Physical Science with Graphic Novels

Physics professor Dr. Jason Ho noticed that many of his first-year physics students found the concept of entropy to be challenging. To address this, he created a laboratory activity using the graphic novel *Max the Demon Versus Entropy of Doom: The Epic Mission of Maxwell's Demon to Face the 2nd Law of Thermodynamics and Save Earth from Environmental Disaster* (Auerbach & Codor, 2017). During a two-hour lab period, students used the graphic novel to " . . . explore multiple definitions of entropy, including an equation, a statistical phenomenon, unavailable energy, and the 'arrow of time'" (Ho, Klanderman, Klanderman, & Turner, 2023, p. 145). Students read and discussed how the chapters of the graphic novel describe and explain the paradigms of entropy used throughout history. The concluding lab activity explored entropy as a statistical phenomenon using six-, eight-, and twelve-sided dice.

Later in this chapter we'll relate the results of a survey Ho administered to his students. For now, though, consider one observation Ho made. After the lab concluded, Ho noticed several students stayed behind in order to read the entire graphic novel. One student remarked, "Why can't all textbooks be [graphic novels]?" (Ho et al., 2023, p. 146).

To be fair, science textbooks have a nearly endless amount of material to get through, and they try to make up for the heavy vocabulary, passive voice, and generally uninteresting text with interesting images, but as we discussed in the last chapter, students usually do not spend the time and effort to connect the ideas in the primary textual flow of the chapter to the concepts and evidence being presented in the sidebars, graphs, and images that are outside that primary textual flow. Often students assume that it is the job of their teachers to connect them with the material in the textbook.

That unexamined assumption often leaves science teachers with two equally unappealing alternatives. One is to use the textbook as a form of reference material and unit guide for the teacher only and not require students to engage with it—instead using direct teaching and videos and a lot of hands-on experiments. A good teacher can engage the students' interest and give those students the experience of discovering knowledge through inquiry and experimentation. But teachers need to generate all the activities and outline the direct instruction by themselves. This is a phenomenal amount of work and requires revising material from scratch year after year as the data and conclusions of science change. In some cases it can also mean that there is less of a challenge for students to engage in the conceptual and foundational material on their own. There is a value to students reading about science (though perhaps not as much of a value when they are reading the writing of a typical textbook).

Alternatively, some science teachers lean in hard on the textbook, assigning chapters to read and including guiding questions so that students can engage their brains more deeply than the passive experience of watching a video, and those teachers try to make the connection for students between the concepts in the book and the hands-on experiments in class. This works well for a few star students but often leaves the teacher with a majority of the class complaining that science is boring.

We don't mean to give the impression by the opening anecdote that graphic novels can solve every difficulty of teaching science completely. But as we see in that example, graphic novels do offer an attractive alternative for full mental engagement without the disconnection and stultifying narrative of a textbook. As a supplement to a solid textbook, graphic novels can engage and excite students, while at the same time giving them the chance to learn to engage in conceptual scientific thinking rather than merely enjoying the spectacle of explosions and shattering bananas frozen by liquid nitrogen without doing the work to understand what those things have to do with the larger concepts in the textbook.

Using Graphic Novels in the Physical Science Classroom

Graphic novels can be used effectively to teach each sub-category of science likely to be taught in middle school and high school. This chapter will consider the affordances and constraints of using graphic novels to teach everything from entropy to gravity. We will also consider how graphic novel biographies can help challenge the historical overemphasis of the stereotypical images of scientists as white males, and highlight the ground-breaking work carried out by women scientists and scientists who are people of color. This diversity may help build interest in science among high school student populations who may not be exposed to many representative role models in science.

Helping Students Understand the Journey of Scientific Discovery

Graphic novels can often leverage storytelling arcs to guide the reader in understanding the full context behind the science, offering a more approachable introduction to concepts than is possible in a standard classroom environment (including the struggle behind solving complex problems, the growth mindset necessary for understanding, etc.) and introducing the full context and scientific method behind many key historical discoveries.

In the graphic novel *Suspended in Language* (2004), Jim Ottaviani and Leland Purvis present not only a biography of Niels Bohr but also a description of his discoveries and theories, combining his words with images like a spinning top, a falling elevator, or a cannon shell piercing a watermelon. In this way, the book can give us Bohr himself explaining his theories along with his analogies coming to life on the page.

Darryl Cunningham's graphic novel *Graphic Science: Seven Journeys of Discovery* (2017) describes the lifelong journeys of seven scientists. One of the scientists whose life is briefly summarized in the book is Antoine Lavoisier, who disproved the contemporary theory about combustion, proved the law of conservation of mass, and developed a forerunner of the periodic table classifying elements all in the course of a long career in science. The book also describes Nicola Tesla, who struggled with many medical difficulties (and had an unfortunately bad business sense), championed alternating current, and designed a remarkable range of important inventions involved with the distribution and use of electricity.

One final example from Cunningham's graphic novel is Jocelyn Bell Burnell, arguably the first person to notice the signals coming from pulsars, and a member of the astronomical team that identified those signals and published their findings. Despite being the second author of that groundbreaking paper, Burnell was passed over for the Nobel Prize (which typically goes to the person who runs the lab, the principal investigator, not the person who actually does the experiments or makes the discoveries). Burnell, however, was doing these experiments against the direct command of her adviser. Yet it was her adviser who got the prize when Burnell was proven right. The graphic novel also profiles one of Burnell's heroes, astronomer Fred Hoyle, who thought about galaxies, the life cycle of stars, and the origins of the universe his whole life. He is most noted for developing a theory (along with William Fowler and others) about how different stages of stellar development can create different elements. He may have been similarly passed over for the Nobel Prize because he publicly criticized the Nobel committee for passing over Jocelyn Bell Burnell.

All of these stories, of course, could have been told in a conventional book. One of the features Cunningham's graphic novel can offer beyond a traditional book however is the way panels represent the passage of time and indicate, for all of the scientists profiled in Cunningham's book, how they kept returning to the same questions over the years. Recurring panel layouts occur when a character in a panel is in a certain position in relation to a set piece (like a window). The same scene then occurs again and again each time the character returns to a certain idea or approach. The reader, in flipping back and forth between the occurrences, notices the differences—for instance, that the character has grown older. In the chapter on Alfred Wegener, for example, Wegener is frequently shown in different panels smoking a cigar in a wide-open room when he gets foundational ideas. In several panels, George Washington Carver returns to the woods when he is reasoning things out. Graphic novels allow such stories to be condensed by picturing that which would require multiple pages to describe.

Even if the reader doesn't notice these specific techniques, the reader still gets the intended impression—that science often involves returning to a question (and reworking the answer) again and again. A teacher with a collection of graphic novel biographies of scientists (see the Appendix or our website, gnclassroom.com, for titles) could assign students to read one and consider breakthrough moments. Was the breakthrough isolated or were there other scientists (and non-scientists) who contributed? How long had the scientist(s) been working on the problem or question before the breakthrough occurred? Did the breakthrough answer more questions than it raised or vice versa? Good graphic novels and reflection by students will help them get past the stereotype of the eureka moment being a flash of inspiration coming from nowhere, rather than the culmination of years or even decades of long-term commitment. Such graphic novels can also emphasize communication and teamwork as well as the deep satisfaction that such discoveries and revelations can hold.

How Visualization Aids Scientific Reasoning

Graphic novels can offer a more intellectually engaging alternative to videos, allowing students to activate their own imagination to fill in gaps between panels, allowing them to more easily back up and reconsider an idea or principle (compare the difficulty of flipping back a page or two and trying to find the right spot on a video, particularly as discussion fodder in class) and presenting multiple explanations or examples to make a concept clear.

For example, in Rosemary Mosco and Jon Chad's *Science Comics: Solar System: Our Place in Space* (2018), on page 17, a character named Fortinbras asks what gravity is. The following two pages offer an explanation. In the first panel on page 18, the spaceship's onboard computer offers a direct textual definition. It defines gravity as a force that pulls things toward each other. The computer further explains that every object in the universe is affected by this force constantly. Captain Riley gives an example that she is attracting every single tennis ball in the universe toward her. An inset image in a circle shows an image of Riley (who is an anthropomorphic dog) and a tennis ball with a bi-directional arrow in between. Fortinbras then worries that gravity might be pulling a hawk from Earth toward them. An inset illustration shows Fortinbras and a hawk with a bi-directional arrow again in between. Riley's tail is wagging indicating an excitement about gravity pulling tennis balls toward her. Fortinbras looks nervous about the possibility of attracting a hawk. In one panel then, we have a textual definition, two visual examples, and two emotional reactions conveyed visually and with humor.

In the following panel, Mr. Slithers, the ship's snake science officer, explains that Fortinbras doesn't have to worry about the hawk because they are a long way from Earth and gravity weakens as the two objects (in this case, Fortinbras and a hawk) get further away from each other. Again, there is an inset panel showing an image of Fortinbras a long way from Earth and the hawk. And Fortinbras looks relieved. Each element of this panel provides another context to help students understand the word *gravity*.

Mr. Slithers then explains that the force of gravity is stronger or weaker not only based on distance but also on the mass of the objects. Mass here is defined textually as objects that have more stuff in them. But then, again, Mr. Slithers gives an example. When we drop a tennis ball on Earth, it falls toward the Earth and not toward us because the Earth has much more mass than a person. An inset image shows a tennis ball in space, a moon, and a bi-directional arrow between them. Labels in the inset panel indicate that the moon has more mass and more pull, and the tennis ball has less pull and less mass. The inset has an image of Earth's moon and not Earth itself. This gives an additional context so that the reader can understand that gravity is not unique to Earth, but applies in all situations with planetary mass.

The story moves on from there, with the ship's computer on page 19 explaining that gravity is what collects dust and material together in the universe and causes stars to form. So the defined term, gravity, is then used to convey an important concept (the collection of dust and formation of stars) in a context other than Earth, making the universal nature of gravity clear.

In a single page, the term *gravity* is used in three sentences and one diagram. In addition, each of the four main panels and five inset panels on that page provides a new context for understanding the concept of gravity. Of course, traditional textbooks or trade books might do the same, but likely they might give a definition, possibly an example or two, then move on to incorporation into a concept. The graphic novel adds the powerful medium of image and links that closely with the explanation to greatly increase the number of contexts in which the word is used. Not all graphic novels define concepts with equal thoroughness, but the graphic novel format offers the possibility.

Since gravity is a foundational concept in physics, teachers might assign students to read a one- or two-page excerpt like this, then could project the image in the classroom and ask the students to explain how the book defines the term. Comprehension of the initial definition of the vocabulary word is likely to be fuller and more accurate with such an activity.

Let's consider one more example. In Jim Ottaviani and Leland Myrick's biography *Feynman* (2011), there is a section that runs from page 198 to 211 that reproduces a lecture that physicist Richard Feynman gave in New Zealand in 1979 in which he was trying to explain a complicated idea in physics so that ordinary people could understand it. As Feynman gives the lecture, with the words of the lecture appearing in word balloons, the background behind him changes to show Newton experimenting with pendulums and sound, James Clerk Maxwell experimenting with fire and magnetism, an illustration of how the visual spectrum and radio spectrum relate to each other, Rutherford's model of the atom, the magnetic strength of an electron, and then, from page 206 to 211, Feynman illustrates his own QED theory. As he speaks in a lecture room, the reader sees pictured behind Feynman images of how photons move more slowly through glass, then through air, then an oscillation diagram of how the thickness of the glass relates to predicting when the photon gets deflected by the glass.

In all, behind the image of Feynman lecturing, there are at least twenty-eight diagrams. Each one illustrates the data or theory behind a single part of his theory and does so in a way that doesn't cause the reader to have to disconnect from the primary narrative flow, consider the image, then go back to the primary textual flow. Rather, the two are smoothly integrated so that the explanation can continue without interruption. In each panel, readers get Feynman's words explaining what the data says or how the diagram works and how it connects to the overall theory. Students reading this section would get a very clear idea of how data and diagrams interact with theory and ideas conveyed by text.

Breaking the Stigma of Science

By presenting science in a supplemental alternative medium to a textbook, teachers may be able to suggest to students the adventure and excitement of finding out something for the first time. To be sure, teachers should also be engaging students in experimentation with new and important results, but it is not always possible to tackle real-world problems in a classroom during a forty-five-minute period. When students ask "Why do we have to learn this? We're never going to use it in real life," graphic novels let teachers show students some of the things about science that are exciting and compelling.

The graphic novel *T-Minus: The Race to the Moon* (Ottaviani, Cannon, & Cannon, 2009) captures the physics (and mathematics and engineering) involved in the race to the Moon between the United States and the Soviet Union. Students can feel the excitement of each milestone on the way, and see how science often involves exploring new frontiers, discovering new ways to learn things, and that even a venture like going to the moon is utterly rooted in the concrete details of everyday life.

Graphic novels can also make science more tangible or relevant to students, and it is important to again highlight graphic novels as an important way to inspire students by showing them role models with whom they resonate. Like the impact that having gender and race diversity in superhero movies has on children, it is similarly important to elevate stories from diverse voices and highlight role models with whom students can identify. Classically of course the stereotype of a scientist is one who wears a lab coat, glasses (or safety glasses), and perhaps is highly socially awkward. In many cases our popular media reinforces these stereotypes (like *The Big Bang Theory* or other movies or TV shows). Graphic novels can actively fight against the stigma of science partially because, unlike movies or TV, they aren't as beholden to mass ratings or popular opinion. Take *The Brain: The Ultimate Thinking Machine*—while the story has some flaws of an overly "cheesy" storyline, some students may resonate with seeing Nour, a curious young woman interacting with a character that is a brain in a container, able to talk with computer assistance. Though it is not an important part of the movement of the story, Nour wears a head covering throughout the book. Not only can students learn some interesting facts about the nervous system, but they also see how Nour asks questions about the brain and learns (while trying to escape a mad scientist). In addition, graphic novels can easily insert real people into a storyline in order to reinforce ideas like "not all scientists wear lab coats." You can read further about some of our discussions of graphic novels and real-world women in technology in the next chapter.

Using Graphic Novels to Teach Physical Science

Next we'll discuss how to use graphic novels in the context of the physical sciences. We will start by considering the physical sciences and how to integrate graphic novels into your teaching, how to bring new contexts in to make mundane material more interesting, and how to use graphic novels to open doors and see new horizons related to cutting-edge issues. Finally, we will consider how graphic novels can help students see the interdisciplinary nature of science.

Even the most well-equipped teachers in one or more physical science fields cannot be expected to have the breadth or depth of knowledge to respond to questions from students who assume their science teacher is the authority about everything from the discovery of the Higgs-Boson to the behavior of planetary orbits near black holes and the internal workings of lithium-ion batteries. Even more so, science teachers whose college focus was on life sciences might know about the effect of chemical contaminants on fish or the behavior of black rhinos in shrinking habitats, but might struggle to answer questions about nuclear fission or how skyscrapers respond to wind shear.

As the number and scope of science-focused graphic novels continues to grow, graphic novels offer an ever-increasing wealth of information to help address the requisite understanding of a rapidly evolving field of science and to help satiate the curiosity of students connected with more and more activity outside of the classroom. In addition, rather than a shallow Wikipedia or Google response, a graphic novel is more likely to allow the student to dig deeper into the subject.

At the beginning of the chapter, we gave a quick summary of a study by Ho et al. (2023). Ho had his students read a graphic novel called *Max the Demon Versus Entropy of Doom: The Epic Mission of Maxwell's Demon to Face the 2nd Law of Thermodynamics and Save Earth from Environmental Disaster* (Auerbach & Codor, 2017). This graphic novel makes full use of the opportunities graphic novels provide. In the page given in Figure 3.1, the images show a demonstration experiment using a fish tank and a transparent barrier. The graphic novel makes it possible for readers to see this setup, process, and results of this demonstration experiment in a single page.

In the first panel, the professor asks Julie to show Max how to calculate odds using a fish aquarium. We see by Max's expression that he is interested. Moving from panel 1 to panel 2, students might notice that the brightly colored and numbered fish have changed position. Clearly their location in the aquarium is constantly changing, both in relation to the tank and in relation to each other. Julie inserts a plexiglass barrier and fish numbered four, three, and two, are on the left side of the barrier and fish one is on the right side, setting the reader up for a lesson in probability.

The graphic novel explores, explains, and clarifies the meaning of the concept of entropy. After Ho's students completed the lab, he asked them to complete a short survey based on their experience. Out of twenty-two students, nineteen either agreed or strongly agreed with the statement "I would recommend an appropriate graphic novel in the teaching and learning of other STEM concepts." Twenty students either agreed or strongly agreed with the statement "I found the graphic novel to be a helpful approach to learning STEM concepts more deeply." Comparing graphic novel reading to other textbook and non-textbook readings, eighteen students either agreed or strongly agreed with the statement "The graphic novel format makes the material more meaningful to me." Clearly, at least for the majority of students in Ho's class, graphic novels offer a useful tool for conceptual learning.

The following semester, Ho used another physics-based graphic novel in his teaching, *Suspended in Language: Niels Bohr's Life, Discoveries, and the*

FIGURE 3.1 *Page 55 from the graphic novel* Max the Demon versus Entropy of Doom *by Assa Auerbach and Richard Codor*, www.maxthedemon.com. Reproduced with permission.

Century He Shaped by Jim Ottaviani and Leland Purvis along with several other illustrators, including Jay Hosler (2004). This class of five students used Ottaviani's book not only to reinforce conceptual content being taught in the course but, unexpectedly, Ho also found that the graphic novel helped students to become attuned to the issues of ethics and justice that the book raises, as well as a grounding in the history of physics. Ho again surveyed the students, this time with open-ended questions. Among the responses were these two quotes from students:

"This [graphic novel] gave me good insights into the life of Niels Bohr, and his discoveries play an important role in the recognition of the physical world. This book provided me with a steady foundation, a stepping stone in my understanding of physics history along with the magnificent impact from early physicists to our daily life." This student used the graphic novel to connect the concepts from physics class to daily life and to begin to develop an understanding of the historical context in physics.

"Niels didn't have the words to accurately communicate the ideas that he wanted to express in lectures. No one had the words to describe quantum mechanics in a way that was widely accepted." This student has made a remarkable connection between the concepts and ideas Bohr was grappling with and the difficulty of trying to explain new concepts before the vocabulary necessary has entered the science world (let alone the wider world). Clearly, the graphic novels that Ho employed added some important elements to his students' learning.

In the following section, we explore three case studies of other ways graphic novels might be directly applied to a classroom context to meet the needs of a range of student learners.

Graphic Novels to Explain: Integrating GNs into a Standard Lesson Plan

Graphic novels that are used as supplementary texts can be integrated into slideshows or handouts in order to enhance and engage students during long explanations or derivations of concepts. An example of this could be the introduction of the model of the atom during a physics or chemistry class. The Rutherford-Bohr model of the atom plays a fundamental role in secondary education as students learn about "molecular orbits," often culminating in activities like a hydrogen spectra analysis lab. However, a graphic novel like the one used by Dr. Jason Ho, *Suspended in Language* (Ottaviani, Purvis, & Hosler, 2009), is useful for explaining this concept and making clear to students that the Rutherford-Bohr model is not the end of their learning. This book, detailing the life of Niels Bohr and the journey of the model of the atom, allows teachers to help students understand how the Bohr model is useful to visualize the atom in a simplified sense and gives them a taste of atomic theory while stressing the difficulties of visualizing it.

A more in-depth use of *Suspended in Language* can be modeled after Fleshman's detailed approach of a weekly reading assignment during a physical chemistry course (Fleshman, 2018). This model facilitated student conversation through weekly guided questions for reading assignments. This discussion-based approach can be taught in tandem with normal classroom activities, particularly if *Suspended in Language* is paired with wavelength calculations in upper-level physics classes, or in energy-level discussions during upper-level chemistry classes. Fleshman split up types of questions into six categories: conceptual, technical, contextual, adventure, survey, and open-ended.

Depending on the age and achievement level of their students, teachers may need to scaffold the process of connecting what they are reading in a graphic novel with what they may be reading in a textbook, but each can enrich the classroom experience in different ways. For example, highlighting contextual understanding can help students connect science to disciplines like history and English. This association may also help students bridge their own interest from their favorite subjects to science. Adventure may increase student motivation and interest. Having students surveying or reflecting upon their experiences could help students engage in metacognitive reflection.

The final category of open-ended questions though, is one that science teachers should pay particular attention to. Because graphic novels are not bound by the regimented structure of a textbook, they are freer to pursue tangential ideas and connections. Asking students what they noticed in the book gives them the opportunity to bring up discoveries and conclusions of their own and lets them experience the increased freedom of scientific research and musings. Such an open-ended question also allows students who might struggle with the calculations and technical aspects of science, as well as the high achievers, be able to have a voice in the class expressing something about science that matters to them. Further, these varying ways of engaging with the graphic novel can reflect the levels of Bloom's taxonomy for deeper learning (Armstrong, 2016).

In addition, integrating a graphic novel like *Suspended in Language* can increase the engagement and appreciation of the complexity associated with classroom concepts and foster a more engaging, relaxed learning environment as students view the physical sciences context in a different light. Furthermore, this book allows students to look behind the curtain and see not only how scientists work with each other to make sense of data and ideas but also what students could explore in further educational opportunities. This might lead to higher numbers of students pursuing opportunities in physical sciences higher education.

Graphic Novels to Enhance: Bringing New Contexts to Mundane Material

Physical sciences, while interesting and engaging, can often be challenged by students as removed from reality. Yet there are an increasing number of careers that require the sort of foundational thinking that such courses provide. Students in physical sciences often struggle to bridge the gap between the fundamental skills they are currently learning and the career objectives where they will apply these skills in context.

Graphic novels can present physical science concepts within the context of careers and jobs in order to stress the importance and application of what is being learned. Take for example *Ichi-F* (Tatsuta, 2017), a manga graphic novel series that details the life of a nuclear cleanup technician after the 2011 Fukushima Daiichi nuclear disaster. Nuclear safety environments follow some of the most stringent regulations of any STEM career path and demonstrate the most extreme cases of how chemical dosages can be calculated and affect the lives of those working in direct contact. The basic safety protocols taught in physical chemistry courses are toned down in comparison to those in the nuclear environments, but nonetheless the focus on personal protective equipment (lab coats, goggles, gloves, etc.) are some of the most crucial elements in the foundations that students will take into their careers.

For example, students with an interest in construction or trades may encounter lead or asbestos and need to understand the importance of their protective equipment in ensuring their safety and career longevity. In *Ichi-F*, there are a few examples where the author does an in-depth discussion of personal protective equipment, and a reader travelling through each panel learns about the individual elements of a protective suit, and why they matter in the context of a highly toxic environment. Integrating a graphic novel like *Ichi-F* into a nuclear chemistry unit during high school or in the preliminary lab safety instruction during any science course can bring a relevance and depth to the material through real-world examples of how this matters. For example, the yearly dosage limits that the protagonist Tatsuta has to abide by, limiting his ability to work, is a direct result of lifetime dosage limits and calculations that can be brought forth and computed using the methods learned in the class. Further, the examples of direct dosage exposure for the protagonist as a result of improper personal protective equipment usage can be a stark reminder of how even the smallest things can make a difference in high-risk environments.

Graphic Novels to Excite: Opening Doors and Horizons to Cutting-Edge Issues

Bridging the gap between what's learned in physical sciences classrooms and what is happening out in the world can be difficult and nearly insurmountable for many teachers. Science teachers may need to field questions on topics occurring in the news like deep fakes in Artificial Intelligence, plans for a human mission to Mars, or rapid advancements in renewable energy. Science topics discussed in the classroom can often feel far removed from the cutting edge of what's being announced on television: reduction-oxidation reactions studied in chemistry were first formulated in the bronze age and quantum mechanics was formulated in the 1920s.

Teachers may often feel unequipped or under-informed about the vast amount of information and scientific progress. It is helpful to be able to direct students to understandable content in order to explain new developments and concepts that extend beyond what is discussed in the classroom. Graphic novels can offer an approachable, vetted medium to introduce students to the larger problems faced in science today, like the impending shift away from Moore's Law, or understanding why the Higgs-Boson discovery is so impactful.

Take *Smash!: Exploring the Mysteries of the Universe with the Large Hadron Collider* (Latta & Weigel, 2017), a graphic novel discussion of the CERN Large Hadron Collider, the facility that confirmed the existence of the Higgs-Boson. This book could be offered to advanced students or groups of students to discuss the standard model of particle physics, unraveling concepts like quarks and gluons, which are often excluded from today's high school curriculum but play a fundamental role in high-energy physics.

Integrating a graphic novel like *Smash* into topics or research projects for students can help stretch their imagination of not only what it looks like today, but also the possibilities of unsolved and exciting problems in the future. Offering targeted materials to students already inclined to specific areas can help them refine their focus and consider possible career paths. For example, older elementary students, middle school students, and high school students alike might be interested in *Astronauts: Women on the Final Frontier* (Ottaviani & Wicks, 2020), describing the struggle that women and underrepresented racial and cultural groups had in being originally excluded from this highly coveted career, and the advances and innovations they achieved once they were allowed to be part of NASA.

Such graphic novels can also increase a student's sense of identity in the sciences, allowing students to enter into the world of the book. The general yet abstract nature of science can lead to the alienation of students, specifically those in cultures that are underrepresented in science communities. A student reading *Astronauts: Women on the Final Frontier*, or *Suspended in Language*, will not only lose themselves in the story but also, often, imagine themselves as the main character or at least as someone living in that world. This reading, especially if it is independent, can do more to reinforce the reasons for entering a science career than all the interesting experiments and lectures a teacher might give.

A student unfamiliar with scientists and how they work might learn from the apprenticeship that a science-focused graphic novel can provide. This could give a solid footing to the layers of different privileges that may be available to many-generation students versus first-generation students who are less likely to know about scientists and what they do.

Applying graphic novels to excite may be the most open-ended application but also one of the most fulfilling and potentially rewarding for a student in how their future trajectory can be adjusted and guided by a teacher.

Applying These Principles to Connect Science to Other Disciplines

Across physical sciences and life sciences there is the need for continuous improvement in how we are breaking down the barriers between science and other disciplines taught in the classroom. Graphic novels by nature of their format can be a strategic tool in order to engage teachers from across English, history, creative arts, and STEM fields, as well as to collaborate multi-modally and encourage interactions that immerse students in content, presenting it within different contexts. With memoirs like *Feynman* (Ottaviani & Myrick, 2011) and *Hawking* (Ottaviani & Myrick, 2019) detailing key historical events and the impact that science has on them, teachers across English, history, and STEM can reference similar passages or illustrations to ground different aspects of the same conversation, like the development of the atomic bomb, the structure of atoms, and the arrival of key scientific minds fleeing from Europe in the face of persecution.

Graphic novels that combine science and fiction are also an excellent way to connect English and Science (and in so doing, engage some students who love reading stories with the sciences, and students who love the sciences with the joys of fiction). The following two examples illustrate how very differently fiction can interact with science. Raina Telgemeier's *Guts* (2019) is a fictionalized memoir of young Raina's anxiety and how that affected her digestive system and vice versa. As Raina goes through medical tests, stress at school, visits to a counselor, difficulty in sleeping over at other people's houses, and worries about speeches in front of class, the reader is reminded again and again about how emotional health, physical health, and mental health are all connected. This might be an interesting trade book to accompany discussions of the gut-brain connection.

While *Guts* is a story that is very much grounded in realism, Jay Hosler's *Last of the SandWalkers* (2015) is a hard-to-classify mix of science fiction and fantasy. The book tells the story of Lucy, a courageous and scientifically insightful beetle, who joins a group of friend beetles (and one dangerous professor beetle) to journey beyond the oasis city where they all live to discover the world beyond, and perhaps learn something about their place in the universe in the bargain. Before long, Lucy is facing seemingly insurmountable challenges and inevitably applying scientific concepts (or adventurous bravery) to overcome them. In this book, like Hosler's *Way of the Hive*, readers soon find themselves caring deeply for the insect characters—itself an important lesson in empathy and perspective.

And, of course, science-based graphic novels can also be applied to the other disciplines grouped under the STEM acronym. Many of the opportunities to apply graphic novels within the context of science form the basis of our conversation in the following chapters on technology, engineering, and mathematics. For instance, the use of graphic novels to help students memorize terms within a life sciences context translates nearly directly to that of rules and regulations for engineering. The utility of graphic novels to engage students in the science context, which students sometimes see as onerous, is equally applicable to mathematics, which often faces a similar challenge. While science textbooks often come across to students as unapproachable and intimidating, graphic novels can significantly diffuse this effect and make science more accessible by key concepts in fresh and multimodal ways, enhancing the classroom experience, and exciting students about the new horizons and opportunities continually opening up in science with our rapidly progressing world. As we will see in the chapters that follow, technology, engineering, and mathematics can all benefit from a similar approach.

Art Notes

One of the consistent themes in this chapter is the idea that science (and perhaps physics in particular) often involves abstract laws and concepts that in order to be understood, need to be rendered concrete—through analogies, examples, or illustrations. We have seen in this chapter how graphic novels do an effective job of this.

Teachers might consider challenging students to provide analogies, examples, and especially illustrations to make such concepts easier to understand. Teachers could start by showing graphic novels that can serve as examples of effective illustrations that help readers understand the concepts or ideas involved. Then a teacher might challenge students (alone or in pairs) to come up with their own images to make the abstract rules, laws, or concepts concrete. If the students then present their illustrations to the rest of the class, the entire class is exposed to multiple explanations of difficult concepts.

This not only helps the students to learn the concepts, but it also offers an opportunity for those who have gifts in art to discover that such gifts have a place in helping people understand science.

CHAPTER 4

Teaching Technology with Graphic Novels

A typical high school student might, in the course of a school day, attend a science class, a math class, and perhaps a shop or engineering class, or at least have an engineering unit in one of their other classes. Students might go to a business class that teaches computer applications like spreadsheets and website design, or they might be taking a course in programming applications, or even attend a robotics club after school. While they will encounter technology in all of their classes including history, English, arts, and physical education (e.g., via presentation software, internet research, word processing, digital design programs, and heart monitors), most students will never attend a course specifically labelled and exclusively concerning technology. Because while technology is everywhere, it is also generally user-friendly enough that it fades into the background and it is often assumed that today's students, as digital natives, will have automatic fluency in it.

The term *Technology* is included in the STEM acronym not only because technology is ubiquitous as a tool in our schools but also because it is often an important part of life or a career destination, especially for mathematics and science students. Students who are interested in math and science may end up programming, engaging in data analytics, or developing new applications for hardware. But what exactly do we mean when we think about technology in schools, and how can graphic novels help us teach that subject if it is not, in fact, usually a separate subject at all?

Technology is perhaps the least well-defined and often underemphasized topic in most education curricula, particularly at the middle and high school levels. Because technology has a fair amount of overlap with the other STEM subject areas, this chapter will consider technology in two ways, first, as a discipline of its own and second, as an element or tool that is embedded within other disciplines.

When viewed as its own area of study, technology serves as more than just a tool but as a broader mindset for progress through discovery and innovation. Although we often interpret technology to mean computer hardware, programming, or even classes in typing, in order to think technologically, students must learn to unpack mysterious processes, reason logically and algorithmically, and trace through multiple iterations on the journey to advancement. Learning to think technologically is a prerequisite for working on the leading edge of technology, which further requires anticipating the directions that technology will evolve and expand across multiple platforms and applications as designers and engineers improve upon user experience. The more mastery students have over ways of thinking technologically, the greater the chance that they will be able to access the most exciting part about technology: determining and taking advantage of opportunities for creativity, innovation, and discovery.

When teachers and students think about technology in the context of other disciplines, they are often considering technology as an application of science more broadly. That is to say, they are defining technology as an understanding of a novel use of science. Most of the graphic novels we will reference in this chapter do this as well. For instance, topics such as cars, robots, and flying machines are all highlighted technological innovations that appear in graphic novels. Further, expertise within this domain includes skill in programming; understanding, assembling, and innovating with existing hardware; and using distributed networks like the internet to source procedures, code, and concepts. Informed by these resources, this chapter takes a broader perspective and views technology as any work with thinking machines. This chapter will extend the foundations of graphic novel application described in the prior chapter on science into a more applied and focused field. Consider these examples to begin:

Box Brown's graphic novel *Tetris: The Games People Play* (2016) includes a history of sports technology from the first rudimentary dice games to the development of the computer game Tetris and its complicated journey from Russia, where it was developed, to the United States where it was mass produced.

Laika (2006), by Nick Abadzis, tells the story of the Russian dog who was one of the first creatures to be launched into an earth orbit, and how the technological development and moral choices led to the dog's successful survival of the launch and initial orbits but also led to its eventual death in orbit. The graphic novel also considers how that knowledge affected its human owners.

Sydney Padua's *The Thrilling Adventures of Lovelace and Babbage* (2015) combines a factual biography of Ada Byron Lovelace and Charles Babbage, who together theorized how a computer might be built, with an imagined narrative of what that computer might have been used for if they had been able to build it.

Ottaviani, Cannon, and Cannon's *T-Minus: The Race to the Moon* (2009) describe the race to the Moon between the United States and the Soviet Union and how newly developed technology, including early computer code, was put to the test.

Each of these graphic novels holds the potential to connect, interest, inspire, enlighten, and offer explanation to readers in ways that the existing curriculum alone may be unable to provide.

Generally speaking, there are three goals that graphic novels can help teachers and learners of technology achieve: *explaining technology*—specifically developing an understanding for the language and mindset of technology as its own discipline; *enhancing understanding of technology*—instruction in the principles and methods of coding; and *exciting students* with a fuller understanding of both historical and big-picture contexts along with bridging student interest from other interests and academic disciplines to technology. We will look at each goal and show how some example graphic novels can make it easier for teachers and students to reach these goals.

Graphic Novels to Explain: Technology as Its Own Discipline

Especially when it comes to communicating technological ideas, graphic novels can be a useful launching pad for building inquisitive curiosity and considering technology as more than just a tool, but as a *mindset*. For instance, if we view technological advancement as the application of science to solve a problem, that leads us to reflect on questions such as "What science do I know?" or "In what ways can I solve the problem in front of me using science?"

With such a narrow perspective, teachers may think that the only technology taught in school is keyboarding, spreadsheets, and web design, each of them instruction on the techniques and processes involved in properly using each of these tools. But with the rapid pace of development in technology, no sooner do teachers use class time to teach the use of a particular program or application, than the program or application is replaced by something new. Thus, it is difficult for such a curriculum to stay relevant. When we develop technology as a *mindset*, then the process of developing technology also includes asking questions of a researcher in any STEM discipline. Especially when considering application in the context of specific scientific disciplines, technology can appeal to students' interdisciplinary interests as well.

One way in which you could use graphic novels to explain technology as a mindset would be to consider the history of technology development. *The Thrilling Adventures of Lovelace and Babbage* (2015) gives a creative introduction to the development of the first design for a computer. This graphic novel begins with a historical biography of Ada Lovelace and Charles Babbage and describes their designs of the Difference and Analytical Engines, complete with extensive footnotes providing direct quotations and historical details. The narrative then takes an innovative turn (together with some creative liberties) to a pocket universe in which history turned out differently. In this imagined version of England in the mid-1800s, Babbage and Lovelace get funding from the queen to build their Difference Engine and are then pressured to use it to fight crime and advance England's position in the world. While amusing to read, this portion of the graphic novel also gives specifics about the components of the Analytical Engine and continues with substantial footnotes detailing the truth behind what might have happened in the pocket universe.

When viewed in this light, *The Thrilling Adventures of Lovelace and Babbage* depicts more than just the invention of coding, but also how humans can take the tools available to our generation and expand the horizons of what is possible. Instead of just focusing on a given output being a decimal or a string in programming code, readers can ask: how is this solving the problem at hand? What further capabilities does it have? Is this idea worth pursuing? How will it affect the way humans live their lives? As students learn to relate to the larger context of the problem under consideration, they begin to develop a technological mindset.

As a second example, we can return to the discussion of *Tetris: The Games People Play (2016)*. Almost any teacher after the turn of the twenty-first century likely has at least one student who professes to "just want to make video games." But as a teacher, you can transform this desire for video games into a constructive force to help students stay engaged in the classroom. Consider a direct quote from Box Brown's book: "Alexy believed that games were the perfect confluence of humanity and technology. Games model the human experience. Not just physically but mentally and emotionally" (2016, p. 67). As Brown explores in the novel why people were drawn to Tetris and, by analogy, are drawn into playing video games, so too can teachers challenge their typical disdain for video games and instead try to steer students into considering what makes video games so entrancing, and how some elements of computer games can be found in many other places including advertising, navigation systems displays, social media, avatars, and more.

A starting point might be to consider the first chapter of *Tetris: The Games People Play*, which discusses the history of games, where they first came from, and why they were created. A teacher in social studies or history could challenge students to reflect on each of these prompts that Brown provides in terms of how the origins of video games affect the form they take and their foundational elements. For example, Tetris involves players deciding between short-term and long-term goals in the game. Can students trace the origin of this in earlier games? Some have argued that Tetris improves spatial reasoning. Were there earlier games that did the same thing? Has there always been an educational or developmental aspect to games? What are some earlier examples of games that improve players' abilities to do specific tasks in daily life?

There are numerous other passages in this and other graphic novels that could explain why technology matters in the context of specific academic disciplines. Some teachers might point out that it is not the responsibility of a class on social studies or language arts or biology to teach technology. We might respond that technology is part of every discipline and making connections across topics and subjects is an important way for students to understand how each academic discipline connects to other ones. Graphic novels are an effective tool to make these connections.

Graphic Novels to Enhance: Principles and Methods of Coding

Now the most obvious way to use graphic novels is for direct instruction (take the earlier example of the very constrained *Tetris*). As we have mentioned before, however, we are not suggesting that teachers replace their regular textbook with a graphic novel, but that using graphic novels as supplements to the text could be very helpful for students at different levels of understanding. Graphic novels are an effective way to enhance students' learning. Graphic novels provide a resource that increases students' engagement without sacrificing attention.

If you are a high school teacher tasked with teaching technology, or even just a teacher who is trying to answer the question of how to help students be prepared for careers in software, what follows may be one small way that you can make a big impact.

Gene Yang's graphic novel series called *Secret Coders* combines an interesting narrative with coding problems that readers can solve. Through the experience of these books, students learn both the principles and techniques of coding and basic computer programming. Books in this series include *Robots and Repeats* (Book 4) (Yang & Holmes 2017), *Potions and Parameters* (Book 5) (Yang & Holmes, 2018), and *Monsters and Modules* (Book 6) (Yang & Holmes, 2018), and we provide short summaries here to illustrate the wide range of topics that are available (all of the books are also summarized in the appendix and can be found on our website, gnclassroom .com).

In the first three books in the series, three middle school students, led by female protagonist Hopper Gracie (a reference to pioneering computer scientist Grace Hopper), get thrown together to solve some mysteries about the academy they attend. They discover that their school has secret rooms, that the janitor is actually a computer professor who is hiding undercover, and that the maintenance robots (which look like bipedal turtles) are programmable. In the first three books in the series, our heroes follow clues left by their teacher (Professor Bee), rescue Hopper's mother (another teacher at the school), and save the school and town from the evil genius Dr. One-Zero. Readers are presented with cliffhanger programming challenges at the end of each chapter to solve before reading ahead in the story. Each book stands on its own and will motivate readers to seek out the other books in the series. Each book also explores multiple aspects of programming. For example, the third book in the series explores Logo programming and allows readers to follow the kids as they save society through computer procedures with parameters and if-else statements.

In book four, the secret coders (Hopper, Eni, and Josh) have found their mentor, Professor Bee, hiding in an underground complex. While he continues to teach them in secret, they also must attend the classes taught by Dr. One-Zero, who is using the students of their school to manufacture his Green Pop which leaves people mindless. So again the coders must save the city, and again it is their coding abilities, along with the amazing hard-light robot, the Turtle of Light, that win the day. The storyline is perhaps a little bit hokey, but this series strongly leverages the narrative story flow of graphic novels to weave together the fundamentals of coding, with challenges for readers to solve in a way that is both funny and engaging. In addition to fourth grade through middle school students who are interested in or open to STEM, older students may also enjoy an opportunity to work through basic coding problems multiple times, at their own pace, and with a clear explanation to supplement the one they learned in class.

The Secret Coders have their hands full in book five. The evil Dr. One-Zero not only has managed to put together enough of his Green Pop formula to enslave the world, but worse, he has control of the Turtle of Light. Professor Bee explains that their only hope is if Hopper, Eni, and Josh can figure out how to use their coding skills to open a portal into another dimension.

As with the other *Secret Coder* books in this series, the story is interesting and the coding lessons are woven into the narrative so skillfully that while you will notice them happening, they seem like part of the story and utterly necessary to do. This is a great book to grab students' attention and interest them in a valuable aspect of STEM at the same time.

In the sixth book, Hopper, Eni, and Josh have opened the portal into Flatland (a fantastic intertextual connection to a well-known trade book relevant to geometry). Now all they need to do is go through it, rescue the second Turtle of Light, bring it back with them, and defeat Dr. One-Zero before he can enslave the world—and before their parents break up the group.

For another perspective, the book could also be used to guide a discussion about ethics. While the two opposed characters, Dr. One-Zero and Professor Bee, come across as fairly one-dimensional, and the stories might initially be viewed as silly, there are ethical implications for the projects that coders choose to work on, the impacts those projects have on society, and how students want to dedicate their time and effort to making the real and virtual worlds better places.

The final book wraps up the series in a satisfying way. This story combines coding with some geometry and does so in a way that is integrated with the narrative, interesting to student readers, and teaches fundamental coding principles while at the same time helping to make student attitudes toward science and mathematics a bit more positive. These books would help explain ideas in any introduction to coding class and connect mathematical ideas to technological applications.

The writer of the series, Gene Luen Yang, is an accomplished and award-winning graphic novel creator. A former high school mathematics teacher and IT director, Yang was named an Ambassador for Young People's Literature by the Library of Congress and has received a MacArthur Fellowship Genius Grant as well as winning the Prinz, Eisner, and Harvey awards for his books. So student readers are in good hands both in terms of his storytelling abilities and his knowledge of computer programming.

The first book in a projected five book series similar to *Secret Coders is Debian Perl: Digital Detective*. Written by Lauren Davis and Melanie Hilario, the first book was published by Oni Press in 2019. As of this writing, no other books in the series have yet appeared. Like the *Secret Coder* series, it is targeted for upper elementary and middle school. There are as yet, to our knowledge, no similar books written specifically for high school students, but new graphic novels come out every day. Check out our website at gnclassroom.com for the latest reviews.

Graphic Novels to Excite: Historical and Big-Picture Contexts

Modern technology relies heavily on distributed intelligence. Computers, robotics, the internet, databases, motion-captured digital film, and other applications often rely on a large team of experts, each responsible for a small part of the whole. In order to bring that project together into a coherent whole, it is important that each member of that team not only understands their own role or part but also understands the overarching objective or context. This requires that those working in technology, in addition to developing a specialization, also grasp the larger project, and beyond that the systems (like the internet and the electrical grid which that project relies upon).

Contextualization—the process of learning the situation and contributing factors surrounding a project—includes understanding the history that helps in establishing the foundational building blocks, motivation, and the prior steps of development. It also includes understanding the connected systems—how the internet, power grid, workforce, and distribution systems, for example, are part of what the project is connecting to and relying upon. Graphic novels can be an effective way of helping students to see the big picture. Of these features, let's consider historical context first.

Graphic novels like Sydney Padua's *The Thrilling Adventures of Lovelace and Babbage* (2015) and Box Brown's *Tetris* (2016) can, in the case of *Lovelace and Babbage* provide historical and theoretical context for how computers were imagined before they were even built and, in the case of *Tetris*, how the business side of applied computers in gaming was an entirely new idea, especially in Russia, and how the idea of intellectual property rights is not a given.

To understand how graphic novels can help provide context for technology, consider students learning a robotics unit. Typically, technology classes might concentrate on the programming of a robot to do a particular task (e.g., the instructions sent to the Mars Rover). A graphic novel like *Robots and Drones: Past, Present, and Future* (2018) can explain and introduce robotics both historically and in terms of how they fit into a larger career and professional world. Even though programming and technological skills are in high demand for many careers, technology curricula often skip over explaining the background and inner workings of such professions. Careers in programming, robotics, assistive communication, networking, data analytics, and others are impossible for students to imagine themselves doing because the processes, skills, problem-solving approaches, and jobs within such fields are unclear, unimaginable, or obscure. This contextualization also demythologizes aspects of technology, letting readers see inside of not only how they work but how they were developed. This makes a subfield like robotics seem less incomprehensibly demanding and more like something in which the high school reader could find a career.

The nature of a graphic novel is that historical contextualization can be conveyed through words, images, and the combination of the two—and more specifically through clothing, setting, speech patterns, and approaches to illustrations like cut-away images of how things work (Boerman-Cornell, 2015).

In *Robots and Drones: Past, Present, and Future*, Archytas's robot bird guides the reader through the history of the development of robots by trying to define what a robot is. There are many types of robots and tasks that robots can do that are often overlooked, and this book includes such details about different configurations of robots, what they can do, how they are made, and how they accomplish what they accomplish. While robotics clubs are excellent for future programmers and engineers, it is easy for students to get so focused on the building and programming of a particular robot to accomplish a particular challenging goal, that they don't ever get the larger picture of the full range of approaches to designing and building robots for different tasks.

Brooks and Flynn (1989) of MIT's Artificial Intelligence Lab, for example, suggested that interplanetary exploration might better be accomplished by thousands of cheap and fairly unsophisticated robots working together to cover vastly more ground than a single, expensive rover. This sort of global thinking was also present when engineers who were focused on getting robots to walk learned that walking depends not upon static stability (in which the robot is always stable—when a six-legged robot, for example, can extend a single leg while using the other five to maintain stability) but upon dynamic stability, in which a bipedal robot is always in the process of falling forward, but the next leg catches that fall and turns it into movement. (See e.g., Aoi et al., 2016.)

Robots and Drones: Past, Present, and Future is a great resource for any student (or adult for that matter) who is interested in getting the bigger picture of the historical context of technology, engineering, mechanics, or how things work.

Graphic novels can also help students develop a sense of the ways that technology functions within larger systems that are linked in a way that is sometimes almost ecological. An excellent example of a graphic novel that helps reveal the systems that we rely on every day is *Hidden Systems: Water, Electricity, the Internet, and the Secrets Behind the Systems We Use Everyday* (2023) by Dan Nott. As of this writing, Nott's book is still forthcoming from Abrams Comic Arts, but we know it will include an extensive and well-rendered explanation of how the internet works. This graphic novel uses both impossibly long-distance drawings that can show a network that would never fit on a photographic image as well as visual analogies that make the idea of a distributed network graspable.

The book will also describe and illustrate the electrical distribution grid, the gravity flow water system for a typical municipality, and other systems. A graphic novel like this can help students begin to think in terms of systemic solutions and approaches rather than singular applications.

Grasping something as complicated as how the internet works is well-suited to the format of graphic novels. Both long-range and close-up images, combined with embedded explanations and panels to effectively show processes allow for a clear illustration. Further, students can much more easily control graphic novels than videos. As we have already mentioned, backing up and rereading a page is easier to find than backing up on a video (where it is harder to land exactly where you need to than on a page). In addition, the reader more easily controls the pace at which the material moves, making comprehension easier (and without voice distortion).

These graphic novels and others contextualize and demystify areas of technology and bring a remarkably imaginative versatility for explaining technology.

Bridging Technology to Other Disciplines and Student Interests

Graphic novels connect to other disciplines in ways that a traditional textbook may not, a factor that is particularly relevant given the interdisciplinary nature of STEM. For instance, because the appendix of *The Thrilling Adventures of Lovelace and Babbage* (2015) includes excerpts from primary documents that were used in writing the graphic novel, this book could be used to bridge these technological lessons to lessons connecting to primary sources in a middle or high school history class. Furthermore, since Ada Lovelace was also the daughter of Lord Byron, the poet, this graphic novel could also be used to bridge student interests in English and literature and mathematics as another way to seek truth in the universe.

One way to incorporate these ideas into the classroom is to draw parallels to such developments with another class. If a social studies class is working on a unit on the Industrial Revolution, a technology class might challenge students to compare the effects of the shift of manufacturing in the early 1990s from individual craftsmanship to factory mass production to the corresponding shift from large computers used only in corporate, governmental, and higher education settings to the development of the personal computer and how society changed as a result.

Technology as a discipline can also excite students and can be used to bridge student interest from one discipline to another, and from outside interests to motivation for school. As mentioned earlier, one appeal of technology is that it involves exploring unknowns, but it also involves anticipating the future. Technology must anticipate both the needs of the future and also ways that current technology might be applied to meet those needs. As science involves taking a step back from data and experiments to consider creatively the larger systems and processes behind things and how they interact, so technology involves creatively considering not only what technologies can do now, but also what they might be able to do in the future. Graphic novels can show this through both fiction and nonfiction.

Technology's ubiquity can also be a way to motivate students. Technology is part of every field and job, from forest firefighting to alternative energy development, to biomedical sciences, to video game development, to rock concert lighting design, to bicycle materials engineering, to space exploration, and more. While discussing computer programming in a decontextualized way might not engage students' imaginations, considering computer programming as part of motion capture in the latest Marvel movie or as a way to help blind people see and those who have lost limbs walk and grasp things could be fascinating to students. Graphic novels can allow students to see the inside of such work and what a job in those contexts might look like.

As a part of this process, it is important to emphasize not only the creative opportunities and uncharted discoveries but also the deep responsibilities and possible dangers that connect with those future opportunities and applications. Graphic novels like Jeff Lemire and Gabriel Walta's *Sentient* (2019), Nathan Hale's *One Trick Pony* (2018), Alan Moore's *Watchmen* (1985, 2005), and Jonathan Fetter-Vorm's *Trinity: A Graphic Novel History of the First Atomic Bomb* (2012) all raise ethical issues that can and should be considered and debated in the context of a technology class. The first three graphic novels in that list do so through fiction—extrapolating what could happen to a society depending on the technology choices we make.

There are many more examples we could list (for further discussion of graphic novels and ethics, see Chapter 5 on engineering), but for now, suffice it to say that ethical perspectives on computing play out all around us, and affect students at least as deeply as the rest of society. Consider the role of algorithms in the spreading of misinformation, the effect of social media on people's self-images, deep fakes and biases within artificial intelligence, and ways in which technology can contribute to or work against the widening economic, educational, and opportunity gaps between people belonging to different ethnic and cultural groups in our world. Discussing these concepts and issues with students can be an important way to draw in students who might not consider themselves interested in programming or computer applications but are very much invested in influencing ethical and moral decisions in programming, for example.

Using Graphic Novels to Address the World Outside School

We have alluded to the advances of our time in technologies such as artificial intelligence, internet search engines, social media, digital connectedness (including wireless communications), and virtual reality. While this list of what are sometimes called *disruptive technologies* will almost certainly be different in a few months or years, one thing that is important is the ability of graphic novels to not only address the past as is the case in many graphic novels but also the present and the future. When dealing with the velocity of technological growth we find ourselves in, it is important to be able to filter out the noise and understand what is real and important.

Jason Silva, a renowned futurist, describes the time in which we are in as "The age of insanity, because everything is instant, all the time, always on, but also kind of insane all at once." A key responsibility for technology teachers is to help students navigate the pace and saturation of the world and understand what they really need to focus on to succeed. Graphic novels can be one tool in the toolbox in order to do this, particularly in providing examples and future-looking outlooks for different technologies or concepts and cementing them in somewhat believable contexts.

A good, free resource for this is *The Ella Project*, which is a series of short comic books centered around highlighting STEM role models for young women. *The Ella Project* tries to show applications of drones, artificial intelligence, hacking, GPS, and other modern technologies to demonstrate how they are used in a practical (yet often contrived) scenario. A resource like this can help students focus on a single technology at a time, whether it be artificial intelligence, blockchain, cybersecurity, or otherwise to exercise their own judgment or analysis in understanding how the technology is important to society and to them.

This series unpacks the concepts in an approachable way, which may just intrigue a student audience to learn more and potentially pursue a career in that field. At the same time, the series highlights different real women, many of whom are people of color, who work in technology today. While the series does not have the depth of a longer graphic novel, it is readily available online with full classroom toolkits, which means we won't go in-depth with applications here.

Before we move on from the topic of the present or the future in the context of technology, it is important to pause and stress that teaching technology, especially with graphic novels, is best suited to building foundational skills and processes rather than focused descriptions of the shiniest new invention. While technologies will come and go, and no one can truly predict which technologies will be the most impactful for the future. The overarching process and mindset for technology as an application of science is universal for students as they progress through their learning journeys. Alongside this journey of building the skills and processes for technology is developing in students the intuition and compass to think through moral questions and the ambiguity which comes with technology.

Considering *The Imitation Game*

The graphic novel, *The Imitation Game* (2016), gives us an excellent example of how graphic novels can connect student interest to technology while also engaging them in discussions of moral questions. Further, this book also demonstrates how graphic novels can support technology courses in general, while providing an entertaining format to learn about the development of computer science, particularly within the tumultuous context of the Second World War and cracking the code of intercepted German messages. Like the film by the same name, *The Imitation Game* describes the life of Alan Turing, told through the lens of Turing's family and friends (such as his mother and his collaborators). It includes scenes from his childhood and education as well as a detailed depiction of his time breaking codes at Bletchley Park during the war and his subsequent work in computer science. Alan Turing is most famous for his role in helping the Allies break the German Enigma code during the Second World War, and this graphic novel provides a richer account of this complicated person's life.

Both Lady Lovelace and Babbage make guest appearances in the graphic novel as Turing illustrates the concept behind *The Imitation Game* (which we now refer to as the Turing Test). To address the question of whether machines can think, Turing proposes a test in which a human receives blind input from both a machine (A) and another human (B). If the receiver cannot determine which of A or B is the machine, then the machine has passed the test.

Turing's test helped establish much of the foundation of artificial intelligence today. *The Imitation Game* serves as an engaging opportunity for students to learn about these complex issues through an engaging, trade book (non-textbook). The book also provides an opportunity to ask one of the central questions of technology—does the ability to create something like artificial intelligence necessarily mean that we should do so, particularly when the implications of such a technological leap are often not clear until after the technology has been implemented? Interestingly, the way that Turing himself was treated by his government and society may itself lend another level to the question of whether humans are emotionally mature enough to wield some of our creations.

The graphic novel also addresses Turing's homosexuality and how the world in which he lived responded to it, including his criminal conviction in England and subsequent court-ordered hormonal treatments that ultimately lead to his death (whether it was a suicide or an accident). Given the potentially triggering content, this book may be more suitable for more mature audiences, and some parents may object to the inclusion of this graphic novel for this reason. However, it also provides an important representation of brilliant historical figures who identify as members of the LGBTQ+ community.

Objections need to be weighed against the positive content and effects of *The Imitation Game*. This story can provide motivation for older high school students who may want to consider careers in computer science, cryptography, and related fields since key concepts (such as the Halting Problem) are introduced that would be later addressed at an advanced undergraduate or graduate level.

One compelling reason to use graphic novels is to excite students about a topic, particularly those who may be overachieving and bored in a traditional curriculum. This graphic novel would be an excellent launch point for a student to explore ciphers and the work of spy networks, the more advanced techniques of modern cryptography such as RSA encryption or the Diffie Hellman key exchange, or even a discussion about quantum computing. Further, *The Imitation Game* highlights how the role of cryptography has changed radically since Turing's death in 1954. The book provides a historical context to the study of the fundamentals of technological development and to help students understand how technology has evolved and changed to where we are today.

Another resource for those interested in more recent advances in technology would be the graphic novel *The Machine Never Blinks* (2020), which provides a history of surveillance and espionage. Such a resource could guide a fertile investigation and discussion into the potential for misuse of technology, and questions of the morality and legality of the way technology can erode both privacy and freedoms mentioned previously.

Graphic novels can also help bridge from a general interest in programming to a more focused interest in specific careers. Likewise, graphic novels can bridge specific career interests to a general interest in programming and technology. Most bridges allow traffic in both directions, after all. The most obvious career connections include biotech (biology + technology) and fintech (finance + technology), but graphic novels can also bridge between subjects like math and tech, business and tech, or astronomy and tech.

For example, consider the overlap of technology with business. As a way of focusing on this application, teachers might use Box Brown's graphic novel *Tetris*, mentioned earlier in this chapter, which is not only an examination of both the coding and development of the popular video game but also the business side of the game's development within the Soviet Union and the initial challenges the creators of that game faced in trying to sell the game to interests outside of Russia. The book highlights the lack of protections for the financial interests of game developers at that time and might serve as a cautionary tale for students interested in innovation. Pairing the reading of Brown's book with a discussion, in which students consider the challenges and dilemmas presented in the book and how they might face similar challenges someday, can intensify student interest by linking it to their own future experiences.

For students who are more interested in space and the technological developments required to safely launch astronauts to the moon and allow them to safely return as well, graphic novels like *T-Minus: The Race to the Moon* (2009) or *Astronauts: Women on the Final Frontier* (2020) include not only the details about the technology but also consider the human struggle involved. Women astronaut candidates proved themselves capable of enduring the rigorous testing required to qualify for the program, and the scientists were excited about how the smaller candidate's lower weight meant less fuel needed to be expended. In spite of this, public relations and political considerations suggested that the heroes that went to the moon (in the 1960s) needed to be Men. It is important for students to consider how science often runs up against such cultural considerations.

As we consider cutting-edge advancements and directions for future technological developments, graphic novels such as those mentioned earlier explore the evolution of technology and the ways in which we shape and impact how it evolves.

Technology and Graphic Novels

Graphic novels can be an important tool for technology teachers to instruct students about the logic behind coding, to contextualize the development of technology and technological systems to encourage more global thinking in technology students, and to strengthen student motivation through bridging between students' interests and technology and between technology and other academic disciplines. This hearkens back to one of the first points we made in this chapter: technology, at least for now, is usually not a separate class but rather a subject that teachers are increasingly asked to integrate into every aspect of the curriculum.

Teaching technology across disciplines can provide a broader disciplinary perspective and that perspective may be able to combat the feeling that technology is something students and teachers alike are constantly chasing after to keep up with. Instead, technology in a disciplinary context presented through graphic novels can help students be confident in foundational concepts that will remain constant even as applications, software, and hardware incrementally change (and hopefully improve) year after year. Graphic novels naturally fit this approach because they tie in that historical context that is always relevant to the discussion in a cohesive manner that will never seem outdated.

Whether teachers incorporate graphic novels directly into their curriculum or simply have graphic novels about technology available in the classroom as a supplement for struggling students, students who need additional challenges, or interested students—graphic novels can provide a huge amount of value to technology education.

Art Notes

This chapter speaks of using graphic novels to connect the ubiquitous topic of technology to other academic disciplines. We have referred to that connection as bridging. Bridging allows students with interests in other disciplines to connect to STEM disciplines through a connecting interest. The arts are obvious bridges. In previous chapters we have spoken about the connection of the visual arts to graphic novels about STEM topics. But the other arts can also be connected—particularly to technology. For example, the performing arts (music, drama, and dance) rely upon technology to provide light and sound. Contemporary light and sound boards are completely programmable and require understanding not only of computer programming but also sound and lighting engineering as well as an artistic sense about colors, music, and sound and how to use it to enhance the performance.

Writing fiction, poetry, essays, novels, and scripts also requires a knowledge of technology. Including a sufficient knowledge of applications like Spellcheck and Grammarly to know when to follow suggestions and when to ignore them (Grammarly, e.g., is designed to produce standard business English—great for writing business letters and reports, but not so good for creative writing).

Finally, more and more artwork combines different forms of art and different affordances that technology can provide. A good artist of any sort should be familiar with both analog and digital tools.

Technology and art are both excellent bridges to connect diverse student interests with the STEM fields.

CHAPTER 5

Using Graphic Novels to Teach Engineering

Graphic novels about engineering include narratives about building the Brooklyn Bridge; developing rockets to allow humans to visit the moon; designing better skyscrapers; the history of aerodynamics, robotics, and drones; and many other topics that describe the excitement of working with a team to design and build things that advance human knowledge, make life easier, and explore new frontiers.

Engineering falls between technology, mathematics, and science. It offers an amazing opportunity for students to connect these disciplines together and at the same time, connect them to concrete challenges rooted in practical situations. Yet engineering is not a subject offered in all high schools. If it is offered, it is often the last STEM subject that students are introduced to, often the one with the fewest courses offered, and the subject that students get the least exposure to. This may be because schools emphasize the importance of learning fundamental subjects like math and science first. Most students only take their first engineering course upon entering college or university. Because of this, it is possible for gifted math and science students to slip between the cracks and never have a chance to investigate a possible interest in engineering.

Graphic novels, however, can get students interested in and exposed to engineering early—for instance, the graphic novel *The Bridge, How the Roeblings Connected Brooklyn to New York* (2018) describes the conception, design, construction planning, obstacles, revisions, political and supply issues, and finally completion of the Brooklyn Bridge. But can graphic novels do more than just increase interest in engineering? Can they help students learn engineering principles and practices of thinking? Can a graphic novel like

The Bridge help engineering teachers and engineering students reach specific engineering learning goals?

In order to answer that question, we need to know the goals of a typical high school engineering program. That can be difficult. Wilson-Lopez et al. (2020) did a content analysis of 117 empirical studies related to engineering argumentation pedagogies and education. These researchers concluded that "Most studies did not . . . report engineering-specific outcomes" (p. 281). There are, however, a few studies that do suggest both pedagogical practices and engineering-specific goals.

For example, Mejia, Drake, and Wilson-Lopez (2015) gave pre- and post-attitudinal surveys to twenty-five Latinx adolescents aged fourteen to seventeen to determine the effect of community-based design activities that seek to give students experience in designing, analyzing, and solving problems affecting their community. Data showed that " . . . the participants' sense of engineering self-efficacy increased after participating in the project" (n.p.) and that authentic experiences like those used in the study have the potential to increase interest levels for Latinx adolescents to engineering as a field. Increased self-efficacy would seem to indicate a stronger sense of confidence about their ability to do engineering problem-solving. So the research affirms that engineering education can benefit from utilizing community-based engineering design activities.

As schooling systems across the world redesign curriculum (a never-ending process) and consider new goals for skills to introduce at younger ages, one focus is for richer science, mathematics, and technology opportunities. An effective way to achieve those goals is to focus on real-world applications, and engineering is a natural way to do that. Curriculum designers have suggested that if engineering concepts are introduced very early, with activities like popsicle stick bridges and paper airplane competitions, elementary and middle school students may be more inclined to delve deeper into science and technology. In order to understand how engineering studies can help shape student's thinking across the STEM fields, we need to define what we consider engineering to be and how we distinguish it from technology and science. We borrow the framework of Leonard and Derry (2011) to make this distinction across three areas: goals, practices, and knowledge.

Goals of Teaching Engineering—Curricula are built around goals. One of the ways to distinguish between science and engineering is to ask what each discipline hopes to achieve. Simply put, the goal of engineering is to fulfill a specific societal need, where the goal of science is to understand a natural phenomenon. Consider this distinction in the context of graphic novels by contrasting similar novels such as *Science Comics: Rockets: Defying Gravity* (2018) and *T-Minus: The Race to the Moon* (2009). While both books cover the history of rockets and outer space, the former focuses on the overarching physics of rockets, while the latter focuses on the specific challenges and needs of a targeted problem—bringing humans safely to the moon and back before another nation does so. Because of this, *T-Minus* views the topic of rockets and space travel through an engineering lens of how to realize a societal goal by overcoming design challenges, while the more fundamental nature of *Rockets: Defying Gravity* focuses on understanding how rockets, gravity, orbits, and trajectories work.

Engineering Practices—An extension of this distinction is that while engineering is, of course, founded within science, a deep understanding of those scientific concepts is not always part of an engineering education. Engineers can focus on conducting tests to validate the behavior of complex systems by applying known formulas instead of deriving all possible refinements of those formulas using fundamental scientific principles. Engineers need to know enough about an object to explain and predict its behavior but don't necessarily need a complete grasp of the underlying natural phenomenon that contributes to or causes that behavior.

Take the use of steel cable bridge construction: an engineer needs to understand tensile strength and the formulas to apply shear and compression forces on various structural elements but doesn't necessarily need to understand the molecular properties of the steel cable, fasteners, and plates or the atmospheric forces that produce the winds which might put stress on the structure. Further, while the engineer has to be able to validate that the bridge will be reliable to carry loads within the conditions it is specified to operate, the engineer does not need to evaluate whether the bridge would be able to do the same under the gravity and atmospheric conditions of Jupiter, for example.

This way of looking at engineering, is, however, an oversimplification. The more the engineer knows about the science behind the context in which a structure, for example, is being built, the more likely that the engineer will be able to more effectively estimate the parameters in which the structure needs to be built.

This highlights one of the biggest opportunities for educators when teaching students about engineering. A focus on the specific details of an engineering problem can lead students to narrow their perceptions in such a way that they ignore much of the underlying science, creating a risk of imperfect application or missing a more effective solution. At the same time, that focus can help students develop a sense of determining what they need to know to address a specific problem and what information is extraneous. Engineering can introduce students to a trial-and-error approach to prototype testing, which is usually more efficient than the more methodical approach used to develop a new scientific theory.

Graphic novels create a natural bridge in this area—while the focus of a graphic novel about engineering may shift, the overarching narrative structure, and storytelling of the subject necessitates the interweaving of engineering with other STEM topics. Because graphic novels often ignore disciplinary boundaries to address topics in a broader way, they can help to better weave STEM as a unified discipline, and help to connect students' knowledge across the gap between science and engineering.

Engineering Knowledge—Engineering knowledge in some senses can be broken into two broad umbrellas, "adapting science knowledge" and "designing knowledge beyond science" (Leonard and Derry, 2011). The previous chapters about science already discussed the idea of adapting science knowledge to other academic disciplines. Designing knowledge beyond science is often outside of what is taught in most high schools. Rules and standards such as maximum design load, best practices, and societal considerations will completely shift the application of science in an engineering context toward a particular problem-based focus.

Once again, graphic novels are a powerful tool for this knowledge in two specific ways: first, the nature of engineering problems benefits greatly from a description in text form and a visual representation of the components of the problem as well. Second, the historical nature of biographical graphic novels provides the context to explain the motivation behind why certain common practices are done today due to precedence. As an alternative to combing through online articles or disjoint and often incomplete videos available online, graphic novels provide a context and holistic structure to provide the background knowledge beyond the standard curriculum to help develop well-rounded engineers.

Such biographical and historical graphic novels also can make clear the excitement and importance of engineering in a way that may make the discipline much more interesting and even exciting for students.

If learning sometimes requires full understanding before applying that learning (e.g., the long process of understanding the limit definition of a derivative prior to applying differentiation rules in university-level calculus), then graphic novels hold a truly powerful position in order to assist in teaching engineering literacy within a bite-sized context, without assuming a paralyzing amount of prerequisites. As students are introduced to the difference between engineering and other closely related fields, they often wonder next how to become an engineer. Instead of explaining how to teach engineering across different age levels, we will focus on applications of graphic novels to assist in the key tenets and frameworks of engineering: structured problem-solving, human-centered applications, and the considerations for decision-making in engineering.

Disciplinary Literacy in Engineering

While extensive research has been done about how mathematicians and scientists write and read, there is much less about engineering. Disciplinary studies (e.g., Shanahan and Shanahan, 2008) begin by determining what professionals and practitioners in a particular field do when they read, then consider how to help adolescent readers begin to learn these disciplinary practices. The goal of this approach is not merely the hope that they will one day get a job in that field but also that learning to think in disciplinary ways prepares students for a much wider range of callings in life.

Typically, such research involves interviewing several experts in a field about their reading and writing practices and what they read, how they read it, what constitutes validity or truth in their field, and what questions they ask as they read. While for this book we did not have time to conduct a full study (and it may be beyond the scope of this discussion), we did talk to three engineers from a variety of subfields and levels of experience. We spoke with Tat, a senior technical leader and environmental engineer with over three decades of experience in his field; Monica, a project manager specializing in building bridges with the civil engineering division of an international company with fifteen years of experience; and Will, an electrical engineer who is in his third year of working for a regional architectural firm.

While these three engineers represent a range of different cultural perspectives, a range of time in their jobs, and a range of subfields within engineering, it is important to note that they cannot stand in for all engineers in all situations. So while this information is not completely generalizable, we are confident that it is a broad enough look to give readers a sense of how professional engineers read, and perhaps some direction for the goals that teachers of engineering on the secondary level might want to adopt in order to apprentice their students into reading, writing, and thinking like an engineer.

We'll review what we learned from them, then consider how graphic novels can help students learn some of the habits of practice that were reflected in the interviews we conducted.

What do Engineers Read?

In his position, Tat reads environmental study reports, design plans (summaries of solutions or proposed remediation plans), and articles from engineering journals and trade publications.

Monica reads design manuals, textbooks, reference books, replicable documentation, and project development reports.

Will reads data sheets and cut sheets that have manufacturer's information for a product and the model number. He also spends a lot of time looking things up in building code books.

How do Engineers Read?

When reading reports, Tat focuses first on the purpose and objectives, and the conclusions. Then he asks himself whether the conclusions and recommendations are supported by the data and analysis presented in the report. When he reads, he is constantly switching back and forth from the big picture to the specifics. He mentally compares industry standards and best engineering practices within the context of the project he is working on. He can depart from industry practices, but only if there is a compelling reason to do so.

When reading design plans, Tat is looking for constructability, feasibility, and operability. He asks himself whether the proposed system can be built within a specific timeframe and context, and once built, if it is reasonable to expect it can be operated and maintained. When he reads, he sees everything as an interconnected system: if one component starts unraveling, then there can be a cascading effect on the whole system's performance.

When Monica reads, she highlights applicable material for the project she is working on. She makes sure she references where her equations and material come from so that others will know *why* she is doing something the way she is. She often rereads project development reports that might take sixteen months for her team to assemble. When she rereads such reports, she doesn't read from cover to cover; instead she adds notations and content as she goes. She describes it as a living document that includes ongoing input and revision from engineers who specialize in structures, geometry, railroads, environmental considerations, traffic flow, community relations, utilities, waterways, and other areas of expertise.

Will is usually looking for a specific piece of information such as the overcurrent protection requirements for an air handler, or the color temperature of a light fixture. He often has to sort through a lot of extraneous information that he doesn't need. In building code books, he is usually looking for a section or paragraph that addresses what he wants to know and then he carefully parses that relevant subsection.

What Counts as Knowledge or Truth in Engineering?

Tat explains that in environmental sciences and engineering, lab studies conducted under a narrow range of controlled conditions have limited value because natural settings are not closed systems. Open systems in the field include large numbers of variables, and it is hard to account for them all. That means that field studies provide more value for understanding how the overall system operates but make it difficult to determine which variables cause which effects. So what Tat looks for are peer-reviewed journals with focused studies that help to explain causality, field pilot studies, and peer-reviewed examples of systems that demonstrate that reliable operations are possible over a wide range of natural conditions.

Because environmental engineering is trying to solve problems well into the future (perhaps a hundred years or longer), successful studies have to take into account future emergent variables. In addition, seasonal and daily changes are important to account for. There can be variations in wastes from manufacturing operations, for example, that depend on the day of the week that the facility performs different operations. In order for a study to be generalizable, it has to take into account a representative range of conditions.

When Tat reads studies or reports, he is thinking of everything in terms of a probability distribution. What is the likelihood that this system or technology will be reliable? What is the likelihood that something might happen to cause it to fail? He asks himself if he is willing to stake his reputation on what he approves.

Monica says that knowledge in her field is predicated upon her own experience in complex situations, what authoritative manuals say, her knowledge of mistakes to avoid, her mental picture about how a solution might apply to a specific situation in the field, and how well the solution can be integrated with the environment, including people who will be affected by the changes. So how she evaluates the worth of a particular thing she reads is very much dependent upon her own experiences as well as the data being presented.

Will points out that the quantity and type of experience are very important. Some of his bosses have twenty-five to thirty years of experience in different electrical engineering fields along with the knowledge that comes with that background. Much of that knowledge comes from experiences in the field with implementing solutions in different contexts. Similarly, Will values feedback from electricians who implement his designs because their different experiences and perspectives help by telling him, for example, if a specified product isn't of sufficient quality or if his drawings were not clear in a particular aspect.

How Can Graphic Novels Help?

We will shortly explain how graphic novels can help explain concepts in ways that acknowledge the complexity of engineering projects in the field, how they can enhance student knowledge of how to read the way an engineer reads, and how they can excite student interest in authentic engineering and encourage a wide variety of students to consider pursuing a career in engineering. Before we do so, though, it is important to understand some ways in which graphic novels are particularly well-suited to connect with engineering.

First, because the graphic novel format so completely integrates image and text, it is remarkably well-suited to show complicated designs and processes while simultaneously guiding readers to know what to look at and how to understand the images. We have discussed this feature at length in Chapter 2.

Second, unlike with a video, readers completely control the speed at which they move through material and can tailor it to their own understanding. Consider the last time you looked at a YouTube video to learn how to do something that was completely new to you. How many times did you have to replay sections of it (or even the whole video) to fully understand the procedure it was describing, sometimes rewatching sections you do not need to see again because it is hard to pinpoint exactly where you need to be. And how many times did you wish the person on the video would talk slower (or faster)? A reader of graphic novels can stop instantly, back up several panels or several pages if necessary, and can proceed at a variable pace depending on how quickly the reader is comprehending the material. The reader can even compare pages from different parts of the novel simultaneously.

And third, readers tend to view the format of a graphic novel as casual or informal. A textbook, in contrast, seems unassailably authoritative or inaccessible. The engineers whom we interviewed emphasized that engineers need to learn to question solutions in light of particular contexts or possible future variables. The format of a graphic novel makes it more open to being questioned, and thus potentially a good training ground for critical thinking. A student might be more willing to ask a question arising out of skepticism when reading a graphic novel than a textbook. This posture of reading is something that secondary teachers can encourage by the use of a graphic novel.

In the sections which follow, we will use the graphic novels *The Bridge: How the Roeblings Connected Brooklyn to New York* (2018) and *Science Comics: Flying Machines* (2017) to showcase how these aspects of graphic novels might be applied in the classroom. These graphic novels and more are also summarized in the Appendix, and we will continue updating our website, gnclassroom.com, with additional engineering graphic novels as they are written.

Graphic Novels to Explain: Unpacking Structured Problem-Solving

First let's examine ways in which graphic novels can explain engineering ideas to students. The graphic novel, *The Bridge*, describes a problem that occurred early on in building the Brooklyn Bridge. While Chief Engineer Washington Roebling anticipated that they would encounter boulders as they worked within the caissons to dig into the riverbed, there were many more boulders than he anticipated. As digging with pressurized caissons of this size was new, they also didn't anticipate the problem of the boulders making the bottom of the caissons sit unevenly on the riverbed and occasionally tipping enough to let the pressurized air out and some water in.

The Bridge shows Roebling first firing a pistol inside the caisson to determine if doing so would result in any explosions or other ill effects of explosive combustion within a pressurized environment. Next, Roebling experiments with different amounts of black powder until he determines how much is necessary to sufficiently break apart the boulders. He does these experiments within the caisson because he needs to make sure there aren't any variables that could not be accounted for in a lab environment. The graphic novel also includes moments in which Roebling had to explain the causes of the problem and the solution to both the caisson workers who were uneasy about risking another blowout, and the board of trustees who were beginning to doubt the entire project.

A graphic novel like *The Bridge* can be used to highlight ways that the methods used by scientists and engineers are fundamentally different due to outcomes, while steeped in similar processes. After students have read *The Bridge*, teachers can use discussion to bring out the distinctive aspects of the engineering design process to give students the opportunity to discover the similarities and subtle differences between the two approaches.

In addition to helping students understand the difference between problem-solving within engineering and problem-solving in the context of science, *The Bridge* can also support another key outcome for high school engineering programs by making clear the process of problem-solving itself. As students learn the designing, planning, building, and implementing stages, teachers can prompt them to notice the tasks that contribute to each phase. Interwoven through these steps is an emphasis on the importance of communication, particularly in bridging any gaps for non-experts such as clients and technical specialists. This may also serve to make engineering attractive not only for those with a passion for building, but also for those interested in learning the field in order to serve as a communication link for all those involved in a project.

Science Comics: Flying Machines (Wilgus & Brooks, 2017) is another graphic novel that can be used to help students understand each of the four stages of the engineering process. As with *The Bridge*, *Flying Machines* can take students out of the classroom and into the field, in this case to learn how the Wright brothers developed their flying machine. Through the lens of this particular book, we will describe each stage of the engineering problem-solving process in more detail:

Understanding Design—In order to articulate their product, Wilbur and Orville needed to answer the question of "What are the issues and shortfalls of the current flying machines?" In the modern context, the advantages of airplanes seem obvious as they have become integrated into daily life. Graphic novels provide the historical context to clarify for contemporary students that the Wright brothers were working in a context where the uses of airplanes had to be imagined. In *Flying Machines*, Katherine Wright, who was the younger sister of Orville and Wilbur, and early innovator Otto Lilenthal discuss the need to improve on the slow, sluggish, and technologically limited balloons of the day by creating faster machines with the ability to set their direction of travel. In a classroom context, conversations like this can bridge the gap and place students back into the context in which conversations were had and provide key examples of what it would have been like to discuss the advantages and disadvantages of an innovation like the airplane. Certainly it could go faster and provide one more control over the destination, but it must have also seemed dangerous to the point of being questionable as a mode of travel. Teachers might pose this question to their students: What are the areas of society today that are in need of a new solution design like the airplane?

Plan—With the desired product defined during design, it's time to consider the options with which to execute the design. As famously outlined in *Some Aeronautical Experiments* (1902), Wilbur and Orville broke down the key difficulties into specific problems to solve; in this case: sustaining wings, power requirements, and balancing/steering. *Science Comics: Flying Machines* excels in demonstrating and walking through the analysis of all three of these areas using a systematic approach. For example, the novel shows Wilbur arguing with Orville and rejecting the parallel advancements in ship propellers and instead proposing new propeller technology in order to fulfill the necessary power and thrust requirements. Students reading this graphic novel could be challenged to systematically outline the needs, constraints, and possible design elements to follow the Wright brothers' plan and apply similar logic to another problem. This practice is particularly useful since the main argument of the power debate between the brothers is covered in the book, but the details are glossed over for brevity, leaving the opportunity for an engineering classroom to fill in the gaps as an exercise.

Build—This is the phase that many students get the most excited for, as it's often the most tactile and engaging. While this step may seem straightforward, once again graphic novels can play a key role in highlighting key subtleties and distinctions in order to enrich student learning. For example, in the case of the Wright brothers building wings, the overall design was adapted from existing gliders and built out in a series of prototypes. One of the key findings that differentiated Wilbur and Orville's product was their systematic fine-tuning of the camber (the asymmetry between the top and bottom surface of a wing) using a homemade wind tunnel. A key point highlighted well here is the Wrights' almost intuitive discovery of how wings provide lift, which contributed to the fundamental scientific understanding of that concept. Sometimes in engineering, existing scientific theory and principles are not sufficient to support the desired engineering, and the initial plan may go awry. In a classroom context, this conversation can be a rich topic for discovery: discussing the actual theory behind wing mechanics, and then comparing results using the camber given in *Flying Machines* across Smeaton's coefficient, the Wright brothers' coefficient, and the lift equation that is used today.

Implement—In the end, the solution needs to work not only to meet the need once, as with the Wright brother's historic first flight, but consistently under varying conditions and pressures. The product or solution must also be acceptable to the client or end user. This is possibly one of the most overlooked but most difficult steps of engineering: to bring a prototype to a full production or operationalized solution.

Near the conclusion of *Flying Machines*, in a scene that takes place at Fort Myer in 1908, the reader is drawn into the storyline and the increasing success of the brothers. Those unfamiliar with the history will be introduced to the first powered aircraft fatality as their prototype was pushed too quickly into production in the hopes of securing an army contract. The crash revealed the fragility of the product, and key failure points that hadn't been accounted for in the increasingly hurried development. When reviewed with students, this story holds a subtle lesson for budding engineers: what is the balance between user acceptance and the ethical obligations of an engineer to deliver a safe, tested product? Such a conversation could lead to a targeted study with students about what the brothers could have done better to mitigate or minimize the accident, and students can then compare it to modern day engineering requirements and practices—some of which still hold echoes of influence from Fort Myer.

One effective classroom activity would be to give students (or student groups) a variety of engineering graphic novels (see the Appendix for more examples) and ask them to determine which of the elements of the design process (design, plan, build, implement) are represented in the narrative and what they can learn from how those elements are shown in the graphic novel.

Graphic Novels to Enhance: Negotiations in Engineering

While we use the term STEM casually as if the disciplines contained within it are part of one unified, monolithic whole, in fact, each of the disciplines within the STEM acronym is unique. Of the STEM fields, engineering is arguably the most immediately responsible to the people within society who are its clients and users. The solution is being built or designed for a specific purpose and specific people to use. There is often a single person or authority who is responsible for signing off or approving the engineering and accepting it as a suitable solution. Graphic novels can instruct how to best ensure that the applications of STEM specifically answer the problems they set out to solve.

Returning to the example of *The Bridge*, this tension between an engineer and a client can be seen at three specific points during the completion of one of the most ambitious and iconic construction projects of its time: during the delivery to the client, while meeting established requirements, and in advocating for the best solution.

Intangible factors of client delivery—When his father, the original holder of the contract, passed away from tetanus prior to the start of construction, Washington Roebling had to regain the client's trust that as chief engineer, he would be able to complete the project on time and on budget.

Client trust is an intangible that is incredibly difficult to impress upon students and future engineers. Recall how earlier in the chapter, Tat, one of the engineers we interviewed, spoke of how, each time he signs off on a project, he is putting his reputation on the line. It can be difficult to help students understand this notion, since the reputations they have in life are relatively short-lived. A graphic novel like *The Bridge* can immerse students in the situation and stakes of the Brooklyn Bridge project, and invite them to see things from the point-of-view of Chief Engineer Washington Roebling, in such a way that it can help students understand the trust issue from the inside out.

Roebling's authenticity, innovation, and pedigree were the qualities that allowed him to keep charge of the project as the chief engineer. Out of these qualities, typically only innovation is taught in the classroom; Roebling knew that the innovative approach to wire manufacture that his company employed resulted in cables of the best quality, and they were a key in his design parameters.

The trust Roebling earned from his workers by working with them in caissons and his storied competence from the war spoke to his pedigree and created a reputation that was above reproach. That reputation allowed him to continue as chief engineer when the project ran into obstacles, exceeded its budget and timeline, and even when Roebling suffered the bends from coming too quickly out of a pressurized environment, was bedridden, and turned the day-to-day management of the bridge over to his wife Emily (who then had to prove herself to both the workers and the board as well—something she accomplished remarkably well). From the first pages of the book, which focuses on Roebling's wartime experience to Emily's moment of facing down the board, teachers can encourage students to reflect on how reputation is achieved and why it is important for an engineer. In short, teachers can ask students what factors outside of the strength of an engineering product need to be developed in order for it to be a success.

Adjusting to meet requirements—The East River Bridge was incredibly challenging to build. Roebling was effectively wading into unknown waters. Take for example the construction of the towers to support the bridge: Roebling ideally wanted to dig the caissons straight down until they rested on bedrock. However, because the project was taking longer than expected, the board of trustees pressured Roebling to cut costs and stay closer to the overall budget (though the project had surpassed the original estimates many times over by that time). Because it was taking longer than expected to reach the bedrock layer, Roebling began to question whether it was even possible to do so. When the board requested Roebling abandon the goal of reaching bedrock entirely, he needed to assess whether fulfilling that request would compromise the project. This back and forth negotiation of approaches to meet the specifications of a project is one of the most difficult struggles as an engineer—learning to work with the client's concerns about cost and completion time (among other concerns) without compromising the overall safety or integrity of the work is a skill that requires years of experience and keen expertise.

In the Manhattan tower example, Roebling had to determine the shear force that would be applied to the tower and the stability of the supports in the sand against winds and current over tens or hundreds of years. Engineers who are rigid and inflexible will often lose clients or contracts. Students need to learn how to say no when it matters, but also compromise, when possible, to find a solution that satisfies safety concerns as well as budgetary and time-based constraints.

In another example, the inclined stays made of steel wire made the East River Bridge six times stronger than it needed to be. When the Haigh wire scandal hit, Roebling deemed that even with the bad wire that was already hanging on the bridge, the cables had a safety margin of five. What would the difference in cable strength have to be in order to make this so? Future engineers must learn to be experts at estimating and be able to rapidly determine (roughly) if a change should be fought against, negotiated, or accepted.

Advocating for what you know is best—The flip side of meeting requirements is knowing when to encourage clients to change a requirement for their own interests. Once again, students can come to understand this by reading *The Bridge.* One section of the book articulates an excellent example of this balance in the choice to increase the amount of steel in the East River Bridge in order to hold significantly more weight, anticipating the future of trains or automobiles being used on the bridge. Of course in hindsight, this seems like brilliance on the part of Roebling as the East River Bridge is still in use over a century and a quarter later almost precisely because of his insight. At the time it was controversial since the bridge was already significantly over budget, but Roebling as chief engineer defended it. Engineers have to act as visionaries to ensure that designs can live on far past when they leave a project. Roebling displayed this insight by increasing steel in a bridge; a computer engineer may do this by anticipating the demands of a program or system twenty years down the road, as is with many Programmable Logic Controller (PLC) systems still in use in factories across the world. When *The Bridge* is used in a classroom, this intuitive vision is the third point that teachers might stress.

This structure outlines a solid engineering unit plan for using *The Bridge* in the classroom. First, students' initial reading of the novel might identify the soft skills (or lack thereof) in Roebling, his father, his wife, and other engineers that made the project successful, or were barriers to its success. These could include presentation skills, servant leadership in working alongside labor workers, or his management skills in building strong assistant engineers to help him even as he fell ill.

On their second pass through the graphic novel, students can pause to note all of the places where Roebling made compromises. Admittedly, these may be few and far between given his stubborn tendencies, but can include his firmness in not electing a new chief engineer after his father died and the adjustments he made when his workers started falling ill due to caisson disease.

Finally, students can take a third pass through the book documenting the different places where instead of compromising, Roebling pushed for what he knew was best (with varying success). This includes his disdain at the awarding of the wire contract to another company. A multi-pass approach to reading (or assigning different objectives to different groups with a chance for each group to report their findings) encourages students to analyze a situation from multiple viewpoints, putting themselves in the seats of various participants. This perspective is key in helping students understand the impacts of their actions and the various ways that as an engineer, it is not enough to just finish a project or build a device; the user has to stay in the center of the process the entire time.

With other graphic novels about engineering, a teacher might choose to have students focus on these general questions:

1. How do the engineers gain or lose the trust of their client in this book? What is motivating each person?

2. How do the words and pictures interact to show how the engineers choose to compromise to address the concerns of the clients?

3. What does the depiction of the characters reveal about their positions? Do the engineers advocate for what they know is best? How is this shown?

4. What else do you notice in the story about the interaction between the engineers and those they are designing and problem-solving for? What is happening in the time between the panels and in the moments that are not shown?

5. What insights can you gather about how engineering works? What should the characters have done differently? What else did you notice in your reading of this graphic novel that relates to engineering?

Graphic Novels to Excite: Engineering for Decision-Making

While the user stays in the center of the process, ultimately the engineer is the one responsible for making sure that a solution is sufficient and defensible.

In an article in the *Boston Globe* about the Cambridge Analytica scandal, Yonatan Zunger speaks of disasters and accidents that changed the face of science (2018). He recalls that chemistry gave us dynamite, which was so horrifying that Alfred Nobel, its inventor, gave a fortune to establish the Nobel Prize, to inspire society to create constructive innovations instead of destructive inventions.

Zunger writes of chemist Clara Immerwahr, who committed suicide the night before her husband and fellow chemist, Fritz Haber, left to introduce the use of poison gas on the Eastern Front of the Second World War. When nuclear bombs destroyed Hiroshima and Nagasaki, many physicists began political activism, some seeking safety in building more weapons, others advocating for peace. Zunger further speaks of unethical experimentation in medicine at Tuskegee, the horrors of thalidomide, and of bridge and dam collapses which caused civil engineering to rethink approaches. He concludes:

> These events profoundly changed their respective fields, and the way people come up in them. Before these crises, each field was dominated by visions of how it could make the world a better place. New dyes, new materials, new sources of energy, new modes of transport—everyone could see the beauty. Afterward, everyone became painfully aware of how their work could be turned against their dreams (p. 22).

Engineering is a profession in which the expectation of ethical duty to society falls upon the individual. Whereas Zunger goes on to analyze the integrated approach of ethics teaching in chemistry and physics in contrast with the approval board system of biology, engineering places the onus on licensed engineers agreeing to an ethical code of practice to ensure that the tools, processes, and structures that they are designing and approving do not jeopardize the health, safety, and welfare of the public (engineerscanada.ca, accessed 2022).

The reckonings described by Zunger can elicit at least two reactions from students: a dismissiveness of the necessity of the task within the context in which it was executed, or a disgust in the sheer horror of overall society in allowing something so gruesome to take place or be conceived. Discussing with students some of the failures mentioned earlier in this section can lead students to realize that since engineers are the interpreters of requirements into design and execution, they have an indispensable role in ensuring that what is built holds to the fundamental principles of integrity, truth, honesty, and trustworthiness—especially because what is built is often difficult or even impossible to unbuild.

The graphic novel *Fallout: J. Robert Oppenheimer; Leo Szilard, and the Political Science of the Atomic Bomb* (2001), illustrates this debate through the historical development of the atomic bomb and its ethics from the perspective of Leo Szilard. We will examine this example in detail here, but there are also other graphic novels that look at these same questions—for instance, *Feynman* (2011) has some sections that consider physicist Richard Feynman's ethical musings on developing the nuclear bomb. And in fact, *The Bridge* (2018) includes a section that considers the ethics of what happens when one of the suppliers of cable to the Brooklyn Bridge puts personal profit ahead of quality standards.

Fallout shows Szilard and his later Russian counterpart Andrei Sakharov realizing too late that once their role of designing and creating such a powerful tool as the atomic bomb was complete, they had little power to stop the atrocities with which their creation would eventually become synonymous. Foundational scientists often must be visionary and naive to the potential outcomes of the phenomenon they are exploring as discussed earlier in this chapter; their aim isn't to create something usable, but instead to understand something fundamental. As Szilard and Oppenheimer's roles switched from understanding a physical phenomenon to engineering a weapon, their naivety became a weakness as they realized the implications of the power they were giving to those with a different perspective and vision for the tool. Engineers must consider the implications of the uses to which their work might be applied.

In *Fallout*, we see Szilard from his pivotal moment of conceiving the nuclear chain reaction that enabled the bomb, through his adamant advocacy when the Germans were defeated and he tried to stop the development of the bomb, all the way to the final plea to not use the bomb in the Pacific Theatre. In the overall narrative of the Manhattan Project this progression feels minor, but *Fallout* demonstrates how Szilard eventually became a champion for arms control and STEM ethics. In the classroom, this stands as a real and parallel case study to modern ethical dilemmas and the responsibility of engineers to ensure that something that should not be designed and built, is not. Alluded to before, this has implications for every field, even those as seemingly harmless as computer programming. Students should be challenged every step of the way to reflect on the ethical implications of an invention. Such perspectives can start conversations around small improvements, like no-step infrastructure in public transportation to ensure that services are delivered equitably to all groups of people regardless of their physical limitations.

The engineer is the authority to ensure that what is designed works and fulfills the purpose of the client. This work begins when the engineer applies the overall design process, integrates the specific wishes of the client, and then finally applies a personal lens to ensure that the product meets the overall guiding principles for a design. The power that this work entails means that while engineers may get to design cool things and play with cool toys, the burden as a key (if not final) decision maker in many cases will fall on them. Graphic novels in their narrative and integrated style are a powerful way of immersing students into the many facets of the specific roles of an engineer in a scenario. Students not only see engineers model how to perform their duties as decision makers, but get to step into those engineers' shoes and imagine what they themselves would do in that situation.

And in addition to helping teachers educate students about the ethics of engineering, graphic novels (as we have seen in this chapter) can be a useful way for teachers to help students reach disciplinary goals in nearly every step of educating the students of today to be the engineers of tomorrow.

Art Notes

As we have seen in this chapter, engineering involves a discursive process of designing, planning, building, and implementing. This sequence might sound familiar to science teachers or math teachers as it has some commonalities to the steps to designing a scientific experiment, as well as the steps to programming or solving a difficult math problem. It also parallels the approach that graphic designers, copy writers, and other applied artists follow.

As an introductory activity to a lesson on planning and experiment, explaining the steps to solving a problem, or engineering a solution, teachers might want to consider offering students alternate options for following these steps. Students could create a brochure, advertisement, or graphic design project that might include interactions with clients, revision, and some of the other aspects of engineering discussed in this chapter.

CHAPTER 6

Teaching Mathematics with Graphic Novels

In *Logicomix* (2009), Bertrand Russell, a famous logician, struggles to determine if mathematics or philosophy has a clearer path to understanding truth. In *T-Minus: The Race to the Moon* (2009), mathematicians and engineers, using slide rules and hand calculations, compute the design requirements, trajectory, and safety parameters to send a team of humans to the Moon. In *Hawking* (2019), Stephen Hawking's life and work illustrate the deep connections between mathematics, astrophysics, and cosmology. The graphic novel *The Imitation Game: Alan Turing Decoded* (2016) highlights both the challenges of cryptography and Alan Turing's life in mathematics. In *Who Killed Professor X?* (2015), a murder at an international mathematics conference challenges readers to solve several different types of mathematical problems to determine the culprit.

In a discipline that some students find confusing or inaccessible, graphic novels can provide an inviting introduction to mathematical ideas and ways of thinking. But they can also do more than that. Teachers or influencers in students' lives often face some of the same common objections or obstacles to student success in mathematics, which commonly boil down to variations of these three comments: "When am I ever going to use this in my life?" or "Math is boring" or "I don't get it." Once again, we can't claim that graphic novels are the silver bullet that will solve all of your student engagement challenges, but graphic novels can be a powerful tool to help connect math to students in some new and effective ways.

Many of the approaches we will suggest are similar to previous chapters: relating math to real life is similar to how we related science to real life, making math relevant is often encouraging students into a mathematical or logical mindset similar to teaching technology. And yet, mathematics is also different in that it is based entirely on a different set of symbols that students must learn not only to interpret, but to connect to abstract concepts. When we speak of engaging students and getting them excited about math, that does not mean trying to overlay a lot of bright colors and dramatic images and hope that will carry students into the real math. Rather it often refers to helping them make a connection and become engaged in mathematics in an authentic way. Essentially, graphic novels, used correctly, may be able to help students who think they don't like math, discover what makes math exciting for some of their classmates.

As we have seen throughout this book, graphic novels offer a range of ways for students to connect to stories that incorporate mathematics and a range of ways for teachers to motivate learning goals. The examples included in this chapter have great potential for use in middle school, high school, and university mathematics classrooms (as do the approaches described in the rest of the book). Because mathematics instruction and student readiness vary so much for these different educational levels, this chapter will consider each of these levels separately. Like the previous chapters, though, many of the techniques and approaches discussed also spill over to other grade levels. Each graphic novel example will illustrate similar techniques to make math more exciting, but teachers will want to consider where their students are in their mathematical preparedness and what specific goals they have for those students. Varying levels of mathematical literacy and interest mean that different graphic novels need to be used differently for engaging (or re-engaging) a struggling student, an apathetic student, or all the way to a frustrated advanced student.

From the start, it's important to note that most of the graphic novels about mathematics highlighted in this chapter are purely focused on mathematics and core concepts. Of course, because there are so many highly distinct topics covered in mathematics, there is less leeway for using more topical graphic novels as we have suggested for other subjects in previous chapters. This chapter (and the extensive appendix, along with our live companion website, gnclassroom.com) should allow teachers to find a graphic novel that could help any type of students in any type of classroom, as well as the subjects in different grade levels or courses, whether a unit about geometry, algebra, statistics, or other mathematical topics.

Finally, if teachers are looking for ways to apply mathematics in authentic or real-world settings, we encourage reading prior chapters, especially those concerning engineering and technology. For example, the mathematics of flight can be seen in engineering, the mathematics of atoms in science, or the logic structures of coding in technology. Graphic novels like *Feynman* or *Hawking* are uniquely poised to subtly insert mathematics as a part of an overarching storyline. Students may need to be guided to realize the strange scribblings inserted into the panels of *Feynman* with his masterful descriptions of quantum mechanics are actually some of the same algebraic equations that they are dealing with in class today.

Before we suggest some example graphic novels and how they might work, we'll consider what the research has to say about using graphic novels in the classroom. Bear in mind that research on using graphic novels in the classroom is a relatively new field, and focus on STEM subjects is only just beginning to develop. We expect these areas to grow a great deal in the next ten years.

Research on Using Graphic Novels to Teach Mathematics

As yet, there has been relatively little research connecting young adult literature with mathematics, and even less focused on graphic novels specifically. At this writing there are two studies that are of interest. Warden (2022) developed a series of lessons using the graphic novel version of *The City of Ember*. She taught the lessons to six developing bilingual students going into grades ten to twelve during summer school in a midwestern American rural community. The lessons taught students to connect the graphic novel and problem posing—a skill identified as an important part of learning mathematics by the National Council of Teachers of Mathematics (NCTM). Warden's study found that for her students, " . . . problem posing from a YA graphic novel was engaging and exciting and led to interesting mathematical findings" (p. 487). She speculates, based on her findings, that problem posing with graphic novels could " . . .be an opportunity for interdisciplinary learning . . . " and " . . .could lead to collaboration between teachers across disciplines" (p. 487).

Ho, Klanderman, Klanderman, and Turner (2023) piloted the use of content-specific graphic novels in a university physics class, in two advanced geometry courses in two different universities, and in a teaching course on middle school mathematical methods. Their study concluded that the graphic novels they investigated could " . . . enhance the teaching and learning of both physics and mathematics at the university level" (p. 149). They further suggest that the same graphic novels might prove useful for high school courses in the same disciplines. This chapter presents field data from high school and university classrooms and considers effective ways to use graphic novels to reach goals that are specific to mathematics-based academic disciplines.

For this overview of graphic novels that connect well to the teaching and learning of mathematics, we will structure our discussion by starting with middle school, proceeding to high school, and finishing with the university level. In part, this approach follows the development of mathematical concepts from whole number and fraction operations, through algebra and geometry, and eventually to courses typically taught at the high school and university levels such as statistics and calculus. In each of these educational-level discussions, all three purposes for using graphic novels in the teaching and learning of mathematics (i.e., explain, enhance, excite) will be highlighted. We will also note cases in which a particular graphic novel may be suitable for multiple educational levels.

Using Graphic Novels in Middle School Mathematics Classes

Middle school is often the point when there is a strong uptick in students struggling with mathematics. As concepts like fractions, multiplication, and algebra are first introduced, students can be confused or even outraged at times. The phrase "Why are there now letters in my numbers?" is not uncommon to be heard in many middle school classrooms. As many teachers know, these are critical foundational concepts which, if not fully internalized, will likely cause students to fall further and further behind as future concepts continue to build on them.

Furthermore, some of these concepts will continue to be pervasive in their future lives. Calculating taxes, take-home pay, weighted averages, halved measurements for recipes, or numerous other regular parts of life all rely on these foundational middle school math concepts. Most mathematics teachers know that there are never enough ways in the universe to explain these concepts in order to get as many students as possible to finally have that "aha!" moment. Students all learn from different media, techniques, and presentations—graphic novels are just different enough from many of the ways traditionally found in classrooms that have the potential to reach just a few more students who need to learn.

Libraries dedicate entire sections to graphic novels and often include those that can serve as resources for later elementary and middle school students. Melinda Thielbar, in collaboration with multiple artists, is the author of a series of Manga Math Mysteries linked to a variety of different mathematical concepts. Some of these books align with elementary school mathematics curricula, including topics such as whole numbers, money, multiplication, and division, but some of them can be helpful in upper elementary and middle school as well.

One title from that series, *The Ancient Formula: A Mystery with Fractions* (2011), offers an example of a graphic novel that might connect to teaching and learning concepts related to equivalent fractions and operations with fractions in later elementary school or middle school, depending upon the mathematical maturity of the students. For younger students who are first learning about fractions, *The Ancient Formula* could be used to *explain* these concepts or perhaps *excite* some of the same students to delve deeper into fractions and related mathematical ideas.

At the middle school level, the same book would help to *enhance* students' understanding of fractions and operations, such as addition and subtraction. The mystery revolves around a secret formula which has been strategically divided into eight equal parts or wedges. The formula's creator has determined that it would be safest to separate the total of eight "eighths" to avoid letting it fall into the hands of someone with evil intent. The main characters gradually accumulate some of these parts and use mathematical reasoning to determine the total area of the missing wedges.

Another graphic novel in this series, *The Secret Ghost: A Mystery with Distance and Measurement* (2010), explores area, perimeter, and measurement involving inches, feet, and yards for rectangular and related geometric figures. The main characters make scale drawings, keeping track of width and length dimensions, as they solve related problems of perimeter and area using appropriate measurement units. Once again, these mathematical concepts are often introduced in later elementary school but may be reinforced, *explained*, or perhaps retaught at the middle school level to students who initially struggled to learn them.

Another book from this series, *The Kung Fu Puzzle: A Mystery with Time and Temperature* (2011), explores the Celsius and Fahrenheit temperature scales and key benchmarks such as the freezing and boiling points of water. This story also involves a secret code that is solved by measuring elapsed time in hours and minutes.

Each of the three graphic novels in the Manga Math Mysteries series offers an engaging story in which the illustrations provide critical images to help the reader to better understand the underlying mathematical concepts. While these graphic novels can offer readers *explanations* of mathematical concepts typically introduced in later elementary school and revisited in middle school, they can also *excite* readers through the surrounding mystery, encouraging them to explore additional mathematical concepts. Finally, these same graphic novels provide a crucial *enhancement* of these mathematical concepts through stories and images for middle school students who have not yet fully mastered these ideas.

Teachers might decide to use the graphic novel with the entire class (which may require a class set of the book) or, if only a short excerpt is to be used, perhaps projecting a few panels on a document camera. It might also be helpful to purchase several copies of the book for your classroom library to have handy for students who are struggling with the specific concepts illustrated in each book or for groups of students to share together. Sometimes a graphic novel *explanation* might click for a student when the teacher's explanation did not—and handing a student a book allows the teacher to avoid spending class time in re-explanation.

Another series of graphic novels that offers potential for use in the middle school mathematics classroom—especially for students who are interested in programming or applying mathematical logic to the context of computers—is the *Secret Coders* series by Gene Luen Yang and Mike

Holmes (the first book was published in 2015, and the sixth and final book in 2018). Although interested readers can find a more detailed discussion of these graphic novels and their links to computer programming using the LOGO language in the technology chapter, this series incorporates many concepts related to geometry and algebra. Middle school teachers looking for ways to motivate their students to delve deeper into mathematical topics that later connect to computer programming will find the entire series of books to be an excellent resource. Some teachers may choose to start a coding club or teach a minicourse during an exploratory week focused on LOGO programming. These books provide storylines that can both *excite* and capture the attention of middle school students.

Among the mathematical concepts addressed in these books are (regular) polygons, vertex angles (both in Book 2), binary numbers (in Book 1), use of variables (all books after Book 1), and "if-then" logic (starting in Book 3). While we argue that this series of graphic novels would also address the other two major pedagogical approaches (*enhance, excite*), it is worth noting that the *Secret Coders* series helps to *explain* several mathematical concepts appropriate for the middle school level in a literary context that works for learners of this age category. A middle school mathematics teacher might bring examples from this series of books from the coding club into the mathematics classroom, a pedagogical strategy that helps to underscore the interconnectedness of mathematics to other STEM disciplines such as technology. These books also introduce students to general problem-solving and quantitative literacy skills that are at the heart of many mathematical arguments.

One more graphic novel linked to a concept typically taught in fifth or sixth grade is *Prime Baby* (2010), written and illustrated by Gene Luen Yang with colors provided by Derek Kirk Kim. A middle school student named Thaddeus has difficulty understanding his baby sister Maddie. After learning about prime numbers in school and their potential use by NASA scientists as a universal language for communicating with alien lifeforms, Thaddeus decides to decode the apparent ramblings of his baby sister. To his amazement, he documents that Maddie's speech patterns appear to follow the sequence of prime numbers from 2 to 19. As was the case with the Manga Math Mysteries, this graphic novel might *excite* younger students to want to explore prime numbers, although some middle school students might appreciate the process of illumination followed by Thaddeus as he seeks to connect prime numbers to his everyday experience.

It is also important to remember that graphic novels can serve an important role as bridges, helping students who think they are not interested in mathematics connect their interest in stories, puzzles, or mysteries (in the case of the graphic novels mentioned earlier) to mathematics and helping them see that math connects to something they love. (See Boerman-Cornell, Klanderman, and Schut (2017) for an in-depth discussion and example of bridging between mathematics and literature.)

Using Graphic Novels in High School Mathematics Classes

Graphic novels aligned with concepts and even entire courses on the high school level are plentiful. For example, *Manga Guides* offer graphic novel formats that explore specific mathematics topics such as solving systems of linear equations with matrices, statistical topics including measures of central tendency and variation, correlation, regression, and the entire first-year calculus sequence. In each case, the images and story contexts provide opportunities to engage the learner and explain more fully (or in a different way) the traditional treatment of these mathematical concepts that are offered in standard textbooks and related learning activities. Teachers may find these graphic novels helpful *explanations* for visual learners as well as those who struggle to master the concepts through traditional teaching and learning strategies.

One school teacher in our study used *The Manga Guide to Statistics* (Takahashi, 2008) in both middle school and high school mathematics courses during a unit focused on measures of central tendency (i.e., mean, median, and mode) as well as graphical displays for numerical data. He observed that nearly all of his students enjoyed the interplay of the images and text, especially those who, like this particular teacher, had prior experience with and enjoyment of *Manga* materials. It is interesting to note that the middle school students seemed more inclined to invest time in this graphic novel than high school students working on comparable mathematics concepts.

Another resource for the teaching and learning of statistics is *The Cartoon Introduction to Statistics* (2013) by Grady Klein and Alan Dabney. This book features dragon-riding Vikings, lizard-throwing giants, and feuding aliens as main characters as a variety of statistical concepts are explored in this image-based format. In order to appeal to a variety of audiences, advanced formulas and more detailed mathematical explanations are available in the "Math Cave". Like the *Manga Guides* to statistics and regression analysis, this book offers readers engaging characters and helpful visual illustrations and *explanations* of many topics typically covered in an introductory statistics course.

There are relatively few books (other than textbooks) that are commonly brought into the mathematics classroom. One such book is Edwin A. Abbott's classic, *Flatland* (1884). However, a graphic novel provides the perfect environment to include images along with the text, as well as the interaction of these two media.

In the introduction to this chapter, we mentioned a graphic novel authored by Thodoris Andriopoulos and illustrated by Thanasis Gkiokas titled *Who Killed Professor X?* (2015). Students with a love of reading will naturally engage with *Who Killed Professor X?*, particularly if they enjoy mysteries and detective fiction. The book is written as a murder mystery in which a group of mathematicians are prime suspects, helping to capture a reader's interest. Along the way, students encounter mathematical challenges from both algebra and geometry in the witness statements. Once again, students will discover applied contexts for these mathematical concepts presented in a highly engaging visual format. The desire to solve the underlying mystery will motivate many high school students to solve the related mathematical challenges, raising their excitement for the discipline in the process. We contend that graphic novels such as *Who Killed Professor X?* will *excite* and motivate students to want to pursue more mathematical learning and potentially choose careers that place a premium on mathematical thinking and problem-solving.

A former student of ours who is now a high school teacher recently used this graphic novel with high school juniors. He shared that students were engaged while interacting with the graphic novel in general. A few students even requested the opportunity to borrow a copy to finish reading during a lunch period. He reports that students who typically enjoy interpreting and reading pictures or images were highly engaged. He also noted that solving math problems in the context of an underlying murder mystery reminded them of similar experiences solving mysteries earlier during the school year. Some students also enjoyed studying links to famous mathematicians, and the teacher reflected that more could be done to incorporate history into his mathematics courses. Overall, the students had positive reactions to this graphic novel and the teacher noted richer discussions of mathematical concepts.

Who Killed Professor X? is a good example to illustrate all three approaches to using graphic novels in the teaching and learning of mathematics (*explain, enhance, excite*). First, the murder mystery story in this graphic novel can be used to *explain* concepts in geometry (including similar triangles and quadrilaterals, congruent triangles, supplementary and corresponding angles, the law of Cosines, the law of Sines, and deductive proof) and algebra (systems of linear equations, distance, the golden ratio, solving inequalities, factoring trinomials, partial fractions, rational and polynomial functions). Each of these mathematical concepts is addressed in one of the witness statements used by the characters in the mystery to establish an alibi. So, at one level, a high school teacher could use a specific witness statement as a learning activity for specific mathematical concepts addressed in high school algebra or geometry.

Who Killed Professor X? can also *enhance* students' understanding of geometric and algebraic concepts. Students who learn best with real-world contexts and literary connections will engage well with this graphic novel. It is not uncommon to view algebra as a set of skills and procedures with few, if any, real-world applications. In *Who Killed Professor X?*, each of the characters are based directly on real-world mathematicians, and solving some of their witness statements requires algebra (such as solving a linear system in order to justify Carl Gauss' innocence), which should help motivate such students to solve problems of this type.

While this graphic novel might be an ideal choice for a student who is struggling to learn geometric concepts, it would also be a great activity for a small group studying collaboratively. Peer input could help a struggling learner, and these witness statements offer engaging contexts for the group of students to solve. Although the solutions to the mathematical prompts are provided at the end of the graphic novel, if witness statements are shared with the class, then students could enjoy attempting to solve the mathematical problems together. Given a class set of the books, a teacher must provide careful guidance on the portions of the book that should be read by students while saving other portions until after the students have discovered the solution on their own.

Finally, since each of the characters is historically relevant as well, *Who Killed Professor X?* can connect to lessons in history or get students *excited* for delving into the progression of mathematical fields and collaborations over time. An activity that would develop students further beyond the graphic novel content would be to have them write their own witness statements corresponding to contemporary (and ideally more diverse) mathematicians.

Using Graphic Novels in the University Classroom

We next consider potential uses of graphic novels in the teaching and learning of mathematics at the college or university level. Since introductory statistics and calculus are commonly taught at this level, the *Manga Guides* books related to these courses and *The Cartoon Introduction to Statistics* are potentially useful for the university context. Students in non-STEM major disciplines, particularly those who enjoy literature and might prefer to learn through visual, verbal, and multimodal approaches and *explanations*, may find these graphic novels to be an important connecting link to the mathematical and statistical concepts.

Biographies of famous mathematicians and scientists may also *excite* university students in their first or second year to consider a major in a STEM discipline. You might recall from the technology chapter that the graphic novel *The Imitation Game: Alan Turing Decoded* (2016) by Jim Ottaviani and Leland Purvis introduces concepts related to computer programming. In addition to computer programming, however, this graphic novel also introduces concepts related to cryptography, much of which is based on ideas from upper-level undergraduate courses such as abstract algebra and number theory. Due to the frank discussion of Alan Turing's homosexuality, this graphic novel might be easier to assign at the university level than at the high school level to avoid parental challenges to the book selection.

Ottaviani and Myrick's graphic novel biography *Feynman* (2011) describes Feynman's education, time working on the Manhattan project, and career as a professor and physicist after the war. Students pursuing a major in physics as an intersection between mathematics and science might be particularly intrigued and *excited* by this graphic novel. The same readers would also learn important mathematical concepts such as three-dimensional coordinate graphs at the same time. Both biographies would serve the purpose of recruiting potential majors in STEM disciplines, including pure and applied mathematics.

An advanced course in geometry, typically offered as part of a major or minor in mathematics, is often a critical component of training for preservice teachers. For that reason, these courses might especially benefit from a comparison of graphic novels with other formats. The course content often includes a teaching unit that delves a bit deeper into the geometry curriculum taught at the high school level, sometimes as a review near the beginning of the course, perhaps offering extensions of concepts such as congruence and similarity to more advanced topics such as the nine-point circle.

Dynamic software packages, particularly those that are open source and provide free access to all users, like GeoGebra, are often used in such courses to offer students opportunities to make and test geometric conjectures. While these are powerful teaching and learning tools, GeoGebra is essentially an "open sandbox." Without careful guidance from teachers to focus their attention, students may have trouble following through with a conjecture. By contrast, the witness statements in *Who Killed Professor X?* offer already-developed mathematical explorations that align with topics in a typical geometry course ranging from similar and congruent figures to the Pythagorean Theorem. These geometric examples from *Who Killed Professor X?* discussed earlier would apply equally well to the standard high school geometry course, as well as to a more advanced geometry course taught at the college or university level.

The witness statements are a natural launching point for geometric extensions to other axiomatic systems in geometry. For example, although the solutions provided in *Who Killed Professor X?* assume a Euclidean geometry model, it would be possible to have students reconsider or reframe one or more of the problems in neutral geometry (i.e., without the Parallel Postulate or a substitute) or a specific non-Euclidean geometry (e.g., spherical or hyperbolic geometry). The university professor may choose to write new witness statements to account for this geometric context, or perhaps assign students the task of extending existing witness statements to non-Euclidean problem settings.

When two of the authors of this book tried this approach in their university teaching, they found the feedback from university students in an advanced geometry course was very positive. In particular, a few students with ADHD mentioned how beneficial this format was for their learning and that they wished that such resources had been available to them when they were learning geometry in high school (though we would caution readers from any generalizations about students with cognitive and emotional differences—research has shown that different special education students react differently to graphic novels).

Students responded in general that they found the story and interplay of graphic images and texts to be very engaging. The use of this graphic novel provided a nice supplement to other learning activities that reviewed and extended the same geometric concepts contained in a total of five of the witness statements.

A colleague of one of the authors of this book used the same graphic novel during weekly labs in an advanced geometry course in a university setting. After initially asking students to unravel the mystery behind multiple witness statements, the professor then challenged students to reevaluate the same witness statements in a non-Euclidean geometric context, as suggested earlier. While challenging, this extension demonstrates the potential ways to use this graphic novel in the teaching and learning of advanced geometry at the university level.

We also highlight *Who Killed Professor X?* as a case study for the ways that mathematical learning can be *enhanced* using a graphic novel. In an advanced geometry course, one of the book's authors discovered that some of her students needed a more in-depth understanding of concepts typically taught in a high school geometry course as well as greater practice in writing formal proofs of geometric conjectures. This graphic novel provided an ideal supplement to other course materials, noting that a total of five of the witness statements directly address geometric concepts such as congruence, similarity, the Laws of Sines and Cosines, and different types of angles. This pedagogical approach addressed the needs of struggling learners, those who needed to review prior material, and those needing a non-traditional learning activity as motivation to devote the necessary effort to learn these concepts more deeply. In addition to researching biographical information about the mathematicians, students gave presentations explaining a solution to different witness statements from the graphic novel.

The students in that particular course were all Math education majors planning to teach on the secondary level. Eighty percent of respondents somewhat or strongly agreed that they found the graphic novel engaging, that the connections between the STEM concepts and the graphic novel were clear, that it provided a helpful approach to learning said concepts, and that they would recommend using an appropriate graphic novel in teaching and learning contexts. These responses not only indicate that the respondents found the approach valuable for their own learning, but they also saw it as being valuable in their future teaching. Additional feedback from students included the following:

- "It was just nice to be presented information in a different way, especially when drawings and humorous dialogue can be added as well."

- "It kept me engaged and I got to learn . . . it keeps students interested and engaged. "

- "I liked learning about all the different mathematicians."

- "STEM courses are very consistent with a day to day lifestyle. Using a graphic novel to learn mixed up the class dynamic a bit."

- "I liked that the medium of a graphic novel really lent itself to combining both the relevant history and biographies and the math concepts."

- "I would consider using a graphic novel in a secondary school . . . Secondary math classes [are] so crucial when it comes to engaging students and helping them enjoy math and love learning."

- "I would absolutely use this graphic novel in my own classroom. I think it would be a great way to engage high school students and get them to view math as a more fun activity than they might otherwise."

- "I think [this graphic novel] would provide a very different approach to teaching math."

Some universities also offer courses focused on the history of mathematics. Conveniently, each of the characters in *Who Killed Professor X?* is a famous mathematician. So this graphic novel can also be used to bring mathematical history connections into another advanced course. For instance, one of this book's authors had students each select a character, research the history and key mathematical contributions for that historical figure, and present a brief biographical cameo during a class session.

One shortcoming of the graphic novel that was noted by preservice high school mathematics teachers who read and analyzed this graphic novel in an advanced geometry course and a methods of teaching mathematics course is that there is little ethnic or gender diversity among the mathematicians. However, a professor could provide a much more representative list of both ethnically and racially diverse, as well as women, mathematicians throughout history as part of this classroom assignment, and use it to discuss why there is such a disparity. In particular, social status limiting individual voice, lack of access to education, and bias in historical recording all likely played a part in the gender and racial composition of most early historically recognized mathematicians. Such conversations can naturally lead into discussions of students' own assumptions about the identities of mathematicians and sharing their own mathematical autobiographies.

One author used this graphic novel in a methods of teaching mathematics course at the university level. Some of these students had already read the graphic novel and analyzed multiple witness statements in an advanced geometry course taken during the same semester, while others had never encountered the graphic novel before. Though again, some students highlighted the prevalence of white males as characters in the story, most agreed that the book could be used effectively in a geometry or algebra course at the high school level.

Here are a few sample reflections related to the use of *Who Killed Professor X?* in a high school algebra or geometry course that were offered by students enrolled in this mathematics methods of teaching class:

- "I would want to incorporate this in my math classroom because of how creative and different it would be for a math classroom. I never experienced anything like this. I think I would rather use it in geometry than algebra, but both would be great. The book acts as an extra resource for students to understand the content in a different, creative way."

- "I also want to connect the ideas that this is a graphic novel about and using mathematics—a direct connection to my own background as an English major. I want students, regardless of how many books we have, to see the value of combining disciplines. Completing the math in this book was fun because it had a story connected to it that was more than just surface level. I could have copied and pasted the problems without the story, and the problems would have been normal, albeit a little more advanced, than we normally complete. But when we combine the elements of English literature and Mathematics, we can create something new and *exciting* that opens a whole new realm of possibilities."

- "I would love to be able to show students these problems, possibly as a once a week activity where I put the book up on a document camera. If I wanted to keep the book hidden from my students, I could use the problems as a challenge problem, maybe at the end of tests, then students have a fun problem to work on while finished with the test."

Other student reflections followed similar themes, noting the ability to connect the graphic novel to both algebra and geometry, in some cases offering specific pedagogical strategies. One student noted that the solutions are provided at the end of the graphic novel, so it might be best to treat this as one would a teacher's edition and to offer students access to the witness statements only. A teacher might choose to read the novel during class, using a document camera to project the images throughout the classroom. Once students have productively struggled with each problem contained in a witness statement, the teacher would have the freedom to offer hints or alternate methods as required. Also, if teachers have purchased a class set of the books, it is within fair educational use policies to photocopy the relevant pages for the students initially before sharing the entire book with them.

Overall, nearly all of these preservice teachers enjoyed reading the graphic novel and most would consider using it in their own classrooms in the future.

Not all schools will have the budget for an entire class set of a particular graphic novel, let alone multiple titles. When prompted to analyze teaching contexts in which only a single copy, a few copies, or sufficient copies for every student were available, these preservice teachers offered helpful strategies for making optimal use of these copies of the graphic novel.

For example, a document camera could be used to share a single witness statement and related problem with the entire class, after the teacher read the main story, sharing key images along the way.

When five or six copies might be available, suggestions were made to form the students into clusters and assign different witness statements to each cluster prior to presentations of potential solutions to the rest of the class.

If each student had a copy of the graphic novel, then students might be assigned to research a mathematician to create a short biographical cameo to share with the class. Again, several preservice teachers argued for the expansion of the list of mathematicians to include more representative and inclusive options such as Mohammed Al-Khwarizmi, Brahmagupta, Ramanujan, Julia Robinson, Emmy Noether, Benjamin Banneker, and many others. Overall, *Who Killed Professor X?* has great potential for use in teaching and learning in both algebra and geometry courses despite its ethnic, racial, and gender limitations.

In summary, there are many graphic novels that could promote the teaching and learning of mathematics at the middle school, high school, and university levels. Some of these graphic novels may best function by *explaining* mathematical and statistical concepts to new learners. Others may work best to *enhance* student understanding of these concepts, particularly for those students who initially struggled or would benefit from a new learning approach. Finally, some of the graphic novels will *excite* students to want to learn more mathematics and its connections to other STEM disciplines. It might prompt them to pursue a degree in statistics or perhaps a multidisciplinary focus in data science linked to one of the other STEM disciplines. If the challenges of solving mathematical mysteries whet students' appetites, then they may decide to pursue undergraduate and graduate degrees in mathematics, eventually leading to teaching, research, or applied work in mathematics.

Art Notes

Some people view mathematics and art as polar opposites (invoking, often the right brain/left brain dichotomy—when in fact, we use both halves of our brains all the time). This dichotomy is deeply false. Artists use math constantly.

Teachers could point out to students the way in which graphic novel artists often separate panels into thirds, often situating the horizon line two-thirds of the way up the panel, and the bottoms of houses or buildings one-third of the way up, allowing the bottom third to be the foreground. Artists then situate characters and actions in ways that break up the horizontal lines at the one-third and two-thirds mark of the panel.

And there is a fair amount of geometry and measuring happening in the design of a graphic novel page. Most graphic novel panels use straight lines to contrast with the curvilinear shapes of people and landforms. These panel shapes are usually rectangular but sometimes include triangles and other shapes (sometimes even circles). In order to lay out the page, say with three equally-sized panels on the top row, a horizontal panel in the middle row, and two panels on the bottom row, the artist must measure the page, and then for the top row, not just divide by three, but factor in the width of the gutters (or frames) that surround each panel. A different calculation is then required for the bottom row.

While most artists can render perspective by eye, the fact is that there is math (even just intuitively) there too. Students can notice vanishing points and the way parallel and converging lines are both used to give a sense of depth.

All of this is a way to remind students that math is all around us and we use it constantly in our lives.

CHAPTER 7

Unanswered Questions and Concluding Thoughts

So far this book has cited research and given examples of how graphic novels may be an effective way of helping students reach important goals within the disciplines of science, technology, engineering, and math. Within each of these academic disciplines, we have discussed the affordances (and some constraints) that graphic novels offer in terms of engaging students in your discipline, enhancing your teaching, and extending learning for students who may be ahead of the class, or those that need more resources to fully understand. We have discussed specific ways to use graphic novels in the classrooms of each STEM discipline and have given you examples and suggestions for graphic novels to use and how to use them.

However, in breaking up our book into discipline-specific chapters, we suspect we have missed some general things that you might still be wondering about. In the pages that follow, we will try to anticipate and respond to the questions we imagine you might still have.

How Do I Find New Graphic Novels About Science, Technology, Engineering, or Math?

There are some approaches to finding graphic novels that might be helpful for you. One approach is to look for other graphic novels by creators whose work you find useful or enjoyable. Our favorites include Jay Hosler, Maris Wicks, Jim Ottaviani, and Gene Yang. But any time we come across a new graphic novel creator whose work we enjoy, we google them and order their other work from the library.

While Amazon can (and will) suggest books that other people who bought the book you are looking up also bought, there is no substitute for a good local bookstore owner or librarian. If you let them know what you are looking for, they will keep an eye open for you.

There are also some very helpful lists you might have a look at. The easiest is the list included in the appendix of this book. Each graphic novel listed there is one that we have read and can recommend. However, since graphic novels come out at a frankly astonishing rate, you might also want to check out our website: gnclassroom.com. It includes reviews of the latest new titles, written for teachers and including what disciplines such books are best for, what age levels will like the books best, a short summary, and an explanation of what material in the book might result in a parent challenge.

Bill also posts images and quotes from graphic novels as soon as he finishes reading them on Instagram as @bbc_onbooks.

How Can I Tell if a Given Graphic Novel Will Fit With My Teaching?

The first step is to think about what goals you have for your students. Do you need them to be more excited or engaged in the material? Do they need help understanding a particular concept? Do they need to know about famous scientists, programmers, engineers, or mathematicians so they can see themselves in those shoes? Do they need additional challenging material to keep them busy while the rest of the class catches up?

Once you know what your goals are (we recommend writing them out on a piece of paper you can use as a bookmark), you should consider whether the graphic novel fits with the age level and rough reading abilities of your class. This is difficult because not only does every student in your class have different interests but they also have different reading levels. In fact, each student has multiple reading levels depending on their prior knowledge of a given subtopic. Fortunately, our website, gnclassroom.com, can get you started by sorting graphic novel titles according to general grade levels (Elementary, Middle, Secondary, and Post-Secondary). It also works pretty well to just read the graphic novel and get a general sense if the book is likely to benefit a few or many or nearly all of your students. Sometimes a graphic novel only benefits one or two students (e.g., a book about wildfires in California might be extremely interesting to a student who is considering going into the science of firefighting, but perhaps would not have universal appeal). Other graphic novels may have limited general appeal, but, when you find the right student, they could be very important to that student. *The Thrilling Adventures of Lovelace and Babbage* (Padua, 2015), (mentioned in both the Technology and Mathematics chapters) is a quirky book, and much like a campy movie, will not grab every student, but the students who do connect with it are likely to connect deeply.

The bottom line is, you know your community and your students, so you will have to make the judgment calls about what will fit best in your classroom and your school.

Should I Consider Using Fiction Graphic Novels in My STEM Classroom?

Graphic novels about STEM cover the entire continuum between nonfiction and fiction. In elementary school, teachers help students distinguish between fiction and nonfiction by saying that nonfiction is factual and fiction is made up (or in some unfortunate cases, teachers define nonfiction as true and fiction as false). In fact, there is a range between factual accuracy and fantasy on the one hand and between truth and falsehood on the other. All narratives are based on reality and all narratives have to base some of their descriptions on supposition.

Let's consider some of the graphic novels we have recommended in the previous chapters. *The Thrilling Adventures of Lovelace and Babbage* (2015), for example, gives remarkably factual (if somewhat irreverent) biographies of Ada Byron Lovelace and Charles Babbage, including primary source documents and extensive footnoting. Partway through the book, however, the book postulates a pocket universe in which the Difference Engine that Babbage and Lovelace were theorizing about actually gets built, and at this point the book becomes fiction (though, at times, a fiction deeply influenced by the facts). Fortunately, the distinction between nonfiction biography and historical fantasy-fiction is clearly defined. So is *The Thrilling Adventures of Lovelace and Babbage* nonfiction or fiction? It is a hard distinction to make.

Or consider Gene Luen Yang and Mike Holmes's *Secret Coders* series. The geometrical and programming concepts taught in the book are mathematically factual. The stories that are built around those concepts, though, involve alien professors, evil masterminds, hypnotic soda, hard-light robots, and many other fantasy elements. Again, though, it should be remarkably clear to most students which parts are factual and which parts are made up.

Scott and Chabot's *Science Comics: Robots and Drones Past, Present, and Future* is a straightforward nonfiction description of different types of robots and drones and how they work. But its narrator is a wooden pigeon from 350 BCE, which may have arguably been the first attempt at building a flying robot, but certainly departs from historical accuracy when it begins speaking and narrating the story. The book is a mostly nonfiction graphic novel with a fictional narrator. Similarly, Schultz, Cannon, and Cannon's *The Stuff of Life: A Graphic Guide to Genetics and DNA* (2009) is a scientifically rigorous explanation of how genetics works in humans, but it is narrated by an alien that looks like a sea cucumber. Hosler's *The Way of the Hive* (2000, 2021) has amazing insights into the lives of honeybees, but in order to most effectively convey that information, the bees talk. Once again, however, the distinction between the factual and the made-up parts of these narratives are easy for readers to distinguish.

And even nonfiction books that do not include fantasy elements, like Tomasi and Duvall's *The Bridge* (2018) and Ottaviani and Purvis's *The Imitation Game: Alan Turing Decoded* (2016), still need to interpret primary source documents to create a narrative, and, in the case of a graphic novel, the artists need to make guesses about what facial expressions the principal characters of the narrative would have made in reaction to events and ideas.

So all STEM graphic novels land somewhere on a continuum between factual truth and interpretation, between nonfiction and fantasy elements.

Whether teachers should use more or less overtly fictional material depends upon the goals they have. Having STEM-based fiction available to students from a STEM classroom library can help pique student interests and engagement. Fantasy narrators can help some students understand some concepts more clearly than a sanitized authorial voice in a textbook would. A purely fictional book like *Who Killed Professor X?* can provide a situated and embodied set of problems that can, ironically, make learning seem more rooted in the world outside the classroom, even though it is made up.

Our bottom line: evaluate each graphic novel according to the affordances and constraints it brings to your goals in the classroom. Do not eliminate a category like fictional graphic novels out of hand. See first what those books can offer students.

Is There Some Sort of Lesson Plan Model I Can Use to Teach With Graphic Novels?

There is too much variation between grade levels and the different STEM disciplines for a generic lesson plan model to be very useful. Consider the planning that would go into a middle grades computer applications building class compared with an AP Physics class, and you will see what we mean. But we can suggest some elements that you might wish to include in a lesson plan that includes graphic novels.

First, start off by defining your goals for the lesson. This is, we are sure, standard practice for any lesson plan, but we have found that defining the goals makes it much clearer how a graphic novel can help (or when a graphic novel might not be the most helpful). A basic question to ask yourself is, are you using the graphic novel to interest and excite the students about a particular topic, to explain a particular concept in another way, or to extend student knowledge about a particular topic?

Second, consider what graphic novels you are familiar with that might help your students reach this goal. Consult the lists we mentioned earlier in this chapter. Once you know which graphic novels you are going to use, that may influence the way you present those graphic novels and how you use them to get particular ideas across.

Third, think about what pedagogical approaches might most easily help your students reach this goal. Would it be useful to break them into smaller groups? Should they read independently and respond to guiding questions that you prepare? Would it be most effective to work through a section of the graphic novels as the whole class? Would it be more helpful to have a discussion or have them turn in a response to what they read?

Consider the nature of the graphic novel in order to get the most out of it. Make sure that students are looking for meaning in the text, the images, and the interaction between the two. When students engage in discussion, it is sometimes helpful to ask them what part of the graphic novel supports the point they are making.

Leave room for inquiry. One of the things that sets apart good STEM teaching from that which is less effective is making time for students to discover things on their own. Perhaps in the discussion leave an extra question at the end asking students what else they noticed in their reading.

Finally, consider how you will include the graphic novel in your assessment. That can be as simple as asking them to respond in writing with a summary or analysis of what they read. Or it could be a matter of including a copy of a panel or two from the reading on a test and asking them to work out the problem or explain what is happening in the scene and how it connects to what you have been learning in class.

As long as your lesson plan is responsive to your strengths as a teacher, your students' interests, and your love for the content, it will be fine.

How Can I Reference a Particular Page or Show Students an Example From a Graphic Novel?

Unlike a regular textbook, you cannot simply read a graphic novel aloud to your class. To do so obviously leaves off the images and the chance to comment on them. If you wish to have your students engage together with a graphic novel, it is vital that every student have access to both the words and the images.

There are several different ways to make sure that all your students are able to follow along with a particular part of a graphic novel as you are discussing it. The first and easiest (though not necessarily the least expensive) is to get a class set of the graphic novel you want to incorporate. This way every student has a copy and by merely giving them a page number, everyone can see. However, sometimes you want to use a page or two and not the whole thing. In that case, you might use a document camera in connection with a smart board or use other means of projecting the page or the spread you wish to discuss.

If neither of these approaches fit what you are doing, you could photocopy a short excerpt, but be aware of restrictions on photocopying, even for educational purposes. It may be more effective to get a class set.

What Are Some Effective Classroom Practices for Teaching Students With Graphic Novels?

Throughout this book we have suggested ways to use graphic novels to excite, explain, and enhance. In so doing, we have described practices that have been shown to work well in the classroom. But there are a few general methods that didn't fit well in any particular chapter. We will describe those here:

Focusing on a Specific Page

There is a lot going on in a graphic novel page. As we mentioned way back in the introduction, knowledge is being conveyed not only through the text but also through body position of characters, facial expression, settings, mood, style of drawing, intersection between text and image, and, particularly in STEM graphic novels, often through examples, analogies, equations, and/or illustrations that appear behind the character. If there is a set of pages that seems particularly germane to the teacher's goal for teaching in that class period, have students turn to those pages (or project them in front of the classroom). The teacher should have a set of questions related to the topic, concept, or idea. These questions should be as open-ended as possible. In fact, we suggest beginning with the extremely open-ended question: "What do you notice in these pages?" Such a question allows students to enter into the discussion with a diminished fear of being wrong (and often the authors of this book have been surprised at the insights that such a question will bring up). From there, use focused questions to help students notice the concept you are concentrating on. This activity also works if a graphic novel is paired with other readings.

Developing Disciplinary Reading Skills

One of the tasks that STEM teachers have is apprenticing students into the language and thinking habits central to their specific discipline. Because graphic novels are not as daunting as peer-reviewed papers, they make a good place for students to start to learn how to read like a scientist, programmer, engineer, or mathematician. With a class set of an appropriate graphic novel, assign students a section to read and specific approaches to engage during that reading. For example, math teachers might encourage students to read with a notebook and a pencil next to them so that they can work out the problems they encounter as they read. Engineering students might be asked to keep a list of safety requirements, client requests, and affordances and constraints of the context based on where the project will take place. Remind them to read the images as well as the text.

Responding to Assigned Reading

Graphic novels can offer teachers a chance to extend the lesson. Often we think of this in terms of handing a graphic novel to a gifted student in search of something to engage them, or a struggling student desperate for another take on understanding the material. But extending can also occur with all students. Assign a section from a relevant graphic novel before teaching the lesson, then ask students how they can bring the knowledge they have gained to bear on the challenge of the next lesson or unit. As they read the graphic novel the night before, students can either take outline notes, paragraph-style notes, or use post-it notes to write ideas, revelations, questions, ideas, and concepts that they wish to bring up in class.

In addition to these approaches, we encourage teachers to share with each other (and us) approaches that work well. Teaching STEM using graphic novels is a remarkably new endeavor. There is much to learn.

How Can I Assess My Students' Understanding of a Graphic Novel?

Remember that graphic novels are tools to help you reach your disciplinary goals for the class. So start with what the goal is. If it is an engineering class and you are using the graphic novel *The Bridge: How the Roeblings Connected Brooklyn to New York* (2018) and your goal is for students to grasp the degree to which engineering is a client-oriented practice, you might ask them to write a summary of three times in the graphic novel when Washington or Emily Roebling had to modify plans or argue for continuing as planned in the face of clients who wanted change.

If you are teaching an introductory technology class and want to use Gene Yang's *Secret Coders* series to help students learn the basic principles of coding, you might require them to solve the challenges in the book and include a one-paragraph reflection about what they have learned, or break up the class into groups, assign each class a programming problem at the end of the chapter to solve, and then have them make a presentation to the rest of the class showing their process and results.

Some goals might be difficult to measure and, even in some cases, impossible to evaluate with a formal assessment. For example, if one of your goals is for students to become more engaged and positively predisposed toward math, offering graphic novel biographies of Bertrand Russell, Alan Turing, and the US and Russian women's space programs to be read for extra credit might be a great choice. But while you could evaluate whether they have read the book (perhaps through a summary or a quiz), you will be unable to determine whether their actual attitude changed (though you can determine whether it appears to you that their attitude has changed). Perhaps in that case, an informal assessment is more important than a formal one.

What if I Only Use One Graphic Novel in the Whole Year?

While we have made the argument that graphic novels can help students reach disciplinary learning goals in all of the STEM fields, we have not suggested that teachers should throw out all textbooks and regular-text trade books and replace them with graphic novels. Using even one graphic novel in one unit over the course of the semester might catch a student's imagination or interest. That one graphic novel might clarify something for a visual learner who is struggling to connect an abstract explanation with a solid image. The one graphic novel might be able to model what scientists, programmers, engineers, or mathematicians do so well that it helps students imagine what it would be like to choose a career in the STEM fields. And, if that one works out pretty well for your teaching, the next year you might consider adding another one.

What if I Don't Have Time to Incorporate Graphic Novels Into My Teaching?

We would never suggest incorporating graphic novels merely for the sake of incorporating them. As we have argued throughout this book, graphic novels can be used as an effective way to reach the disciplinary goals that teachers have for their students. A graphic novel may be an effective way to reach those goals—so much so that incorporating one may actually save you time.

But if you cannot spare the time at all because of the demands of covering a certain amount of a textbook or trying to make the most of limited lab time, you might consider including graphic novels in your classroom library.

Not only can they help bridge student interest into STEM, they can also help explain concepts that they may not have caught in class. They can also provide high achievers with extension and enhancement when they master concepts that are taking another student longer to grasp.

What if My Principal, Department Chair, or Superintendent Doesn't Think Graphic Novels Are Legitimate Books? What if Parents Object?

Happily, attitudes about graphic novels are changing in the United States. While Europe, Asia, and much of the rest of the world have long recognized the power of graphic novels to communicate effectively using the intersection of words and images, the United States, the United Kingdom, and Canada have lagged behind. Graphic novels have won awards like the Pulitzer Prize, the Newbery Medal, and the National Book Award. Graphic novels have been best sellers and have gained critical acclaim. But the bottom line is graphic novels are effective tools for teaching and are a way to reach students effectively. You could make these points to your administrator.

You might want to enlist the support of other teachers both in and out of the STEM fields and also your school librarian.

And we have found that for every parent that might object, there are usually two others who have seen how much graphic novels have changed their children's attitude toward reading.

And, of course, we would be remiss if we didn't suggest that you might want to give them a copy of this book and have them read at least the first chapter.

What If I Have Been Using Graphic Novels for a While Now and, While I Found This Book Helpful, I Have a Couple of Other Ideas About How to Teach Effectively With Them?

We are always excited about new approaches. If you would like to share your successes, ask us questions, or recommend a graphic novel for us to read, we would be delighted to hear from you. You can connect with us through our website, gnclassroom.com, where you will also find reviews of STEM-focused graphic novels, graphic novels that might be useful for other disciplines, and young adult literature in general.

What Final Words Do You Have for Stem Teachers?

We began this book with a dedication to the high-school- and middle-school teachers that ignited our interests in science, technology, engineering, and math—and more than that in learning and discovery, and the ways that imagination can result in testable theories. Here at the end of this book, we want to thank our readers for the important work they do as teachers every day. It is our hope that graphic novels will strengthen and extend that good work and allow STEM teachers to engage more students, explain to those students more clearly, and challenge those students to consider what part STEM subjects can have in their lives.

Art Notes

One last word about connecting art to the STEM disciplines. The arts can help us remember one of the most important qualities of each of the STEM fields—namely that they contain beauty. One way of thinking about the arts is that while they create products (sculptures, paintings, drawings, songs, symphonies, essays, poems, short stories, novels, plays, dances, and more), the real aim of art may be to help us see in new and different ways.

The truth of the matter is that each of the STEM fields contain deep beauty. Science shows us the intricate ways that all aspects of our world are amazingly put together and connected to each other in dynamic and exciting ways. We see beauty in mountains and molecules, erosion and entropy, the stars and the sea, photosynthesis and epigenetics, and so on. Technology allows us to see planets in orbit around other stars, send rovers to Mars, fly to the upper reaches of the atmosphere and the deepest depths of the sea, and in each of these places we find new and amazing beauty. Engineers build bridges, skyscrapers, airplanes, and robots that not only accomplish important goals and make life easier but do so in ways that are often aesthetically pleasing. And in mathematics we can see the beautiful consistency of the universe.

Perhaps graphic novels can remind us of the important fact that science, technology, engineering, and mathematics each contain worlds of beauty in them.

APPENDIX

Suggested Graphic Novels for Use in STEM Classrooms

Science

Chemistry

Cunningham, D. (2017). *Graphic Science: Seven Journeys of Discovery*. Oxford: Myriad. *Graphic Science* presents biographies of chemist Antoine Lavoisier, proto-paleontologist Mary Anning, botanist George Washington Carver, physicist and engineer Nikola Tesla, geological theorist Alfred Wegener, physicist Jocelyn Bell Burnell, and astronomer Fred Hoyle. This graphic novel shows how science developed over 200 years by focusing on these seven lives. Each biography includes the subject's social, cultural, and political contexts to highlight the way science contends with societal response to theories and discoveries. It is a fairly good graphic novel, though it does not make as much use of moment-to-moment transitions as it might and sometimes seems to function more like an illustrated picture book, just with lots of panels. The light this book shines on the lives of scientists with whom many students might not be familiar is admirable. Having said all that, it is a fascinating book and well worth a read.

Einhorn, H., Staffaroni, A.; & Harvey, J. (2021). *The Curie Society*. The MIT Press. Three new students at Edmonds University receive a secret code leading to an invitation to join the clandestine Curie Society. Through collaboration and application of their unique expertise, they help the leaders of this group to foil an evil plot. The book does an excellent job of demonstrating growth mindset (e.g., learning through making mistakes) and the power of collaboration. It is also a really fun read that will get upper elementary and middle school students excited about science.

Koch, F. (2019). *Bake Like a Pro*. First Second. Young Sage is assigned to study with a senior wizard named Korien, who is an alchemist and a baker. Sage is horrified at first because she cannot see how baking could possibly be magical. As she learns from Korien (through a lot of trial and error) how to bake cakes, chocolate chip cookies, banana bread, cheddar biscuits, pie crust, sponge cake, and more, readers learn along with her. Along the way they learn safety, proper kitchen etiquette, how to clean up, and even some of the science behind why baking works. By the end, readers will come to realize that "Baking is a tangible form of magic." (p. 4)

Murphy, A., & Murphy, L. (2020). *Corpse Talk: Groundbreaking Scientists*. DK Publishing. This collection of eighteen biographical sketches provides an excellent introduction to a diverse group of scientists from a variety of different STEM disciplines, including astronomy, physics, paleontology, geography, medicine, evolutionary biology, chemistry, botany, computer science, and mathematics. Unlike some biographical overviews of famous scientists, which tend to favor males of European descent, this graphic novel includes four females (Maria Sibylla Merian, Mary Anning, Ada Lovelace, and Marie Curie) and two males of color (Al-Haytham and George Washington Carver). Each biographical sketch is about six pages with interactive panels that invite the reader to learn more about each scientist's contributions. In turn, readers may be prompted to undertake a deeper study of the work of this scientist and perhaps pursue the subject matter in greater detail. This graphic novel would be ideal for middle school students wishing to explore both the breadth of the STEM disciplines and a total of eighteen individuals who made important contributions to these disciplines over the past two millennia.

Ottaviani, J., & Purvis, L. (2009). *Suspended in Language: Niels Bohr's Life, Discoveries, and the Century he Shaped*. G.T. Labs. This graphic novel gives a biographical summary of Niels Bohr's life. Starting with his work on surface tension, through the award-winning Bohr model of the atom, until his contributions to the Copenhagen interpretation of quantum mechanics, and finally ending with the founding of CERN. The book is heavy on anecdotes about Bohr's life, particularly in the first half, and points out Bohr's eccentric ways of communicating at many points.

Tatsuta, K. (2017). *Ichi-F: A Worker's Graphic Memoir of the Fukushima Nuclear Power*. Kodansha Comics. This book provides an overview of the cleanup of nuclear power plants after the Fukushima disaster. Focus is given to the mundane tasks that labor workers undergo, including the use of protective equipment and the monitoring of radiation dosages.

Earth Sciences

Chad, J. (2016). *Volcanoes: Fire and Life*. First Second.
Aurora lives in a future world where the world has been blanketed in an
ice age and humanity must survive by burning the ruins of their former
civilization. While scanning a library, Aurora's little sister Luna discovers
a book about volcanic activity and begins to discover not only what got
humanity into this mess, but also what might help them survive it and thrive
again. The answer is geothermal heat from volcanoes. Along the way, of
course, the reader gets a comprehensive understanding as well. This book is
an interesting introduction to the science of volcanology and, more broadly,
geology. A great way to grab student interest.

Cunningham, D. (2017). *Graphic Science: Seven Journeys of Discovery*.
Oxford: Myriad. *Graphic Science* presents biographies of chemist Antoine
Lavoisier, proto-paleontologist Mary Anning, botanist George Washington
Carver, physicist and engineer Nikola Tesla, geological theorist Alfred
Wegener, physicist Jocelyn Bell Burnell, and astronomer Fred Hoyle. The
idea here is to show how science developed over 200 years by focusing on
these seven lives. The books show them in their social, cultural, and political
contexts to highlight the way science contends with societal response to
theories and discoveries. It is a fairly good graphic novel, though it does
not make as much use of moment-to-moment transitions as it might and
sometimes seems to function more like an illustrated picture book, just with
lots of panels. The light this book shines on the lives of scientists with whom
many students might not be familiar is admirable. Having said all that, it is
a fascinating book and well worth a read.

Reed, M. K., & Hill, J. (2019). *Science Comics: Wild Weather: Storms,
Meteorology, and Climate*. First Second. Chase McCloud, a clueless news
anchor, has said one too many ignorant things about the weather and
meteorologist Norman Weatherby has had enough. While reporting on
an upcoming blizzard, Chase makes fun of global warming and Norman
decides to teach him a lesson—literally. He has the technicians cue up a
powerpoint he used when he was a guest at a middle school and proceeds to
explain to Chase about the layers of the atmosphere, how the atmosphere
protects us, how the seasons work, why temperature changes on the planet,
how water and air currents affect the weather, storms and other weather
events, and much, much more. This is an entertaining story packed with
excellent explanations of why our weather is the way it is. While Chase
never quite gets more than a hint of a clue, young readers will find the
story clear and interesting and they will learn a great deal. The images and
explanations sync perfectly and the cartoonish style is goofy enough to be
fun but realistic enough to convey explanations about weather in ways that
are accurate and uncluttered.

Life Sciences

Cunningham, D. (2017). *Graphic Science: Seven Journeys of Discovery*. Oxford: Myriad. *Graphic Science* presents biographies of chemist Antoine Lavoisier, proto-paleontologist Mary Anning, botanist George Washington Carver, physicist and engineer Nikola Tesla, geological theorist Alfred Wegener, physicist Jocelyn Bell Burnell, and astronomer Fred Hoyle. The idea here is to show how science developed over 200 years by focusing on these seven lives. The books show them in their social, cultural, and political contexts to highlight the way science contends with societal response to theories and discoveries. It is a fairly good graphic novel, though it does not make as much use of moment-to-moment transitions as it might and sometimes seems to function more like an illustrated picture book, just with lots of panels. The light this book shines on the lives of scientists with whom many students might not be familiar is admirable. Having said all that, it is a fascinating book and well worth a read.

Cunningham, D. (2010). *Psychiatric Tales*. Bloomsbury. This book is a series of eleven stories as remembered by the author from his time working in a psychiatric ward. He describes the dementia ward and its inhabitant, a patient who cuts herself to relieve anxiety, a schizophrenic homeless patient, depression, anti-social personality disorder, self-harm, bipolar disorder, suicidal tendencies, and more. The emphasis throughout these stories is on the dignity of human beings and how we should recognize that those who have mental illnesses are people with illness rather than subjects of ridicule and disparagement. Cunningham's job gives him an interesting perspective. He spent enough time caring for his patients, that he developed concern and caring for them. Because he is not a doctor, he doesn't need to distance himself emotionally in the same way doctors do in order to make clear decisions, and because he is not a family member, he can take a kind of outsider's perspective to the patients. The result is a remarkably insightful book. Cunningham's art is sparse and simple, but effective. The book is in black and white which works well to highlight the devastation that the various mental illnesses can cause, but it also lends a quiet dignity to the patients he is depicting.

Einhorn, H., Staffaroni, A., & Harvey, J. (2021). *The Curie Society*. The MIT Press. Three new students at Edmonds University receive a secret code leading to an invitation to join the Curie Society. Through collaboration and application of their unique expertise, they help leaders of this group to foil an evil plot. The book does an excellent job of demonstrating growth mindset (e.g., learning through making mistakes) and the power of collaboration. It is also a really fun read that will get upper elementary and middle school students excited about science.

Fies, B. (2006). *Mom's Cancer*. Harry Abrams. This graphic novel takes the reader from the moment that the author's mother had a small seizure and discovered she had a tumor growing in her brain, through how her three children (called in the book Me, Nurse Sis, and Kid Sis) walk with her through brain scans, diagnosis, waiting, understanding the depth of the problem, first appointments with doctors, biopsies, chemo, side effects, radiation, stages of grief, miraculous healing, and life after cancer. The book is at least as much about how siblings cope with the illness of a parent as it is about the author's mom's journey. The art is an interesting combination of caricature and realism. This may be a good one for a teacher to have handy for a student struggling with a parent's cancer.

Flood, J. (2018). *Sharks: Nature's Perfect Hunter*. First Second. While the narrative story here is pretty thin, mostly involving counteracting the myths we have about sharks, the book is still jammed full of amazing questions like these: Sharks don't have bones, so how do they make red blood cells? Sharks don't have flotation bladders like fish; how do they control their buoyancy? The book also contains interesting facts like: Hammerhead sharks can see a range of 219 degrees. The book uses the conventions of graphic novels to show us processes like how sharks breathe, give birth, and other natural processes.

Frederick-Frost, A. (2020). *Grow a Garden!*. First Second. This graphic novel gives details of how to create your own at every stage in the process. From selecting the right seeds and creating your own potting soil to transitioning seedlings outdoors and choosing planters, this book walks through each activity along with safety instructions.

Hirsch, A. (2019). *Cats: Nature and Nurture*. First Second. Bean the Kitten is a star of countless cat videos but takes time out of her busy schedule to describe everything you ever wanted to know (and some things you didn't know you wanted to know) about the anatomy, behavior, and distinguishing characteristics of pretty much every variety of domesticated and wild cat on the planet. With Bean as our guide, and Hirsch's mastery of panel movement providing the structure, readers will enjoy learning about cats and exploring their world.

Hirsch, A. (2017). *Dogs: From Predator to Protector*. First Second. While this looks like a book about dogs (and to be sure, the book covers different species, behavior, and other things) it actually uses dogs to discuss genetics including selection, recessive and dominant traits, fossil records, evolution, domestication, migration, the development of eyes that can perceive depth, color blindness, how dogs hear different frequencies than we do, smelling acuity, communication, history of dog breeds, and other topics. Rudy the dog is our guide to all of this information and he is an excited, enthusiastic, and likable narrator.

Hosler, J., Cannon, K., & Cannon, Z. (2011). *Evolution: The Story of Life on Earth*. Hill and Wang. An alien scientist named Bloort 183 (who looks a bit like a one-eyed starfish mounted on a stack of inner tubes) has just put the finishing touches on the Glargalian Holographic Museum of Earth Evolution and is giving a tour to King Floorsh 727 and his son, Prince Floorsh 418 and on this tour, Bloort explains how different life on Earth is than it is on Glargal where all life reproduces asexually and without variation. The result is a remarkably interesting and remarkably in-depth book. Hosler uses this contrivance of aliens trying to understand life on Earth (as Mark Schultz, Zander Cannon, and Kevin Cannon did with the earlier book in this series, *The Stuff of Life: A Graphic Guide to Genetics and DNA*) as a great way to explain complicated scientific ideas without too much jargon and in a way that offers a full explanation without insulting the readers' intelligence. It also allows for an overarching story that we can escape to every now and then when the scientific explanations get too heavy. Hosler and the Cannons (who are not related by the way—they met in art school because they have the same last name and found that they collaborate rather well) also include a fair amount of humor which helps the science go down easier.

Hosler, J. (2015). *Last of the SandWalkers*. First Second. Jay Hosler is the amazing biologist/graphic novelist whose first work, *Clan Apis*, follows two worker bees that are part of a colony. In *Last of the SandWalkers*, Hosler here gives us a much fuller story of several beetles who leave their safe home and go out into the desert on a voyage of discovery. Lucy is the plucky leader. Professor Bombardier is her resourceful mentor, Raef is a robotic firefly, and Mossy is a relatively huge horned beetle. Along with them is treacherous Professor Owen. As they journey on what turns out to be an epic adventure, the reader learns a great deal about entomology in general and beetles in particular—including about trap-door spiders, whirligig beetles, and what it is like to get caught in amber. Not that the learning gets in the way of the story—which has enough twists and turns and moments of danger to easily keep students' attention.

Hosler, J. (2003). *The Sandwalk Adventures*. Active Synapse.
Readers learn about the theory of natural selection while listening in to a conversation between two mites that live on a hair follicle of Charles Darwin's beard. Somehow he can hear them and he explains his theory to them. The book not only includes an excellent explanation of Darwin's ideas of natural selection but also addresses many of the most common misperceptions of basic evolutionary theory.

Hosler, J. (2000, 2021). *The Way of the Hive/Clan Apis*. Harper Alley Originally released in 1998 as *Clan Apis*, *The Way of the Hive* is an amazing journey through the life of a honeybee. We follow Nyuki through metamorphosis, meeting her mentor, Dvorah, learning to find and gather honey, learning to communicate through movement the location and direction of pollen, defending the hive, losing Dvorah, and coming to terms with the end of her life. The science is impeccable and the story is remarkably moving.

Howard, A. (2017). *Dinosaur Empire*. Amulet Books. Ronnie, a fifth grader, fails her quiz on dinosaurs and needs to retake it the following day or face the prospect of being excluded from future educational opportunities including college. She encounters Ms. Lernin, a neighbor with a time tunnel disguised as a recycling bin. Using science magic, the two travel back in time to the Mesozoic Era, with stops along the way during the Triassic Period, the Late Jurassic Period, and the Cretaceous Period. Concurrent with the exploration of the animals present during each time period, the development of the land masses on Earth (from Pangaea to the current arrangement of the continents) is illustrated. A key quote from Ms. Lernin is "We have to be ready to accept new discoveries, even if they change the way our favorite dinosaurs look, because that's how science works!" (p. 71). As expected, Ronnie becomes an enthusiastic supporter of all things scientific and eventually aces her re-quiz.

Howard, A. (2019). *Mammal Takeover*. Amulet Books. While playing outside in the snow, fifth grader Ronnie once again encounters Ms. Lernin. This time, a snow fort houses a compost container that serves as a time tunnel, via science magic, to the Cenozoic Era. This most recent (and current) era includes three periods (Paleogene, Neogene, and Quaternary) and multiple epochs. Ms. Lernin emphasizes that even she does not try to memorize the names of the epochs (and instead has a handy multi-color tattoo on her arm to serve as a cheat sheet).

Howard, A. (2018). *Ocean Renegades!*. Amulet Books. Fifth grader Ronnie is invited by Ms. Lernin to visit the local aquarium. This eventually leads to the use of a garbage can as a time tunnel via science magic to the Cambrian period about 500 million years ago. As the two characters visit successive parts of the Paleozoic Era, they explore the animal and plant life that exists in the oceans and the beginning of plant and animal life on the land which is initially barren and desert-like.

Keller, M., & Fuller, N. R. (2009). *Charles Darwin's On the Origin of Species: A Graphic Adaptation*. Rodale. We don't know if this book contains the whole text of *Origin of the Species* or if it is an abridgment, but there is a lot of Darwin's original book here. Normally, this would be a daunting book for a high school student to try to take on—with difficult vocabulary and lengthy and complicated sentences—but, the graphic novel version provides support in understanding through the images. Although Keller and Fuller don't take full advantage of what the graphic novel format can do (e.g., most panel-to-panel transitions move to a completely different subject, instead of using moment-to-moment transition to engage the reader more in the story), and although the art is certainly competent but not spectacularly engaging, nonetheless, it is an engaging book that should help high school science students connect to what Darwin was trying to say. If you teach science and want a good way to connect your readers with a fuller understanding of natural selection, this book would be a good one to have in your classroom.

Kerbel, D. (2021). *Fred & Marjorie*. Owlkids. *Fred and Marjorie* follows the journey of Frederick Banting as he develops insulin to treat diabetes at the University of Western Ontario. The book details at a high level the iterative process it took to isolate the chemical that was refined into insulin and get it accepted into the scientific community as a treatment.

Koch, F. (2017). *Science Comics: Bats: Learning to Fly*. First Second. There is a single narrative through-line about a little brown bat and a teenage girl who initially is not so interested in what the ranger has to say, but when the bat gets close to the group and one of the panicked humans swats it, the girl decides to help the bat in any way she can. But woven through the narrative is plenty of explanation and exposition about nearly every aspect of a bat's life including flight, echolocation, habitat, food, adaptations, threats, and more.

Kwan, G., & Song, D. (2018). *Squidtoons: Exploring Ocean Science with Comics*. Andrews McMeel. Squidtoons takes a whimsical and image-based interpretation to target key misconceptions that young readers may have around specific marine life (e.g., sharks, whales, squid, etc.).

Loux, M. (2017). *The Time Museum*. First Second. Delia is a science nerd. Her thorough report on the life cycle of the dung beetle puts her class to sleep, including the teacher. When her best friend deserts her for a cooler friend at the beginning of the summer and she finds out she and her family are going to visit her eccentric uncle, she takes it in stride. It turns out that her uncle is the curator of the Earth Time Museum and he is offering her a summer internship. She has to compete with other science students for the position, most of them from the future. Can she succeed? This isn't hard science, but throughout the book is that scientific thinking, passion for science, and problem-solving ability are more important than memorized facts, a concept that might be very encouraging to some young science students.

Ottaviani, J., Cannon, Z., & Cannon, K. (2004). *Bone Sharps, Cowboys, and Thunder Lizards: A Tale of Edward Drinker Cope, Othneil Charles Marsh and the Gilded Age of Paleontology*. G.T. Labs

This book tells the story of the bone wars. What happens when two dinosaur hunters, eager for the money eastern museums are offering, compete with each other for the greatest find, oblivious of the cost their feud may have for science? This is a fascinating story that contains lessons about the ethics of discovery.

Ottaviani, J., & Wicks, M. (1996). *Primates.* First Second. Ottaviani profiles three famous women scientists, all protégés of Louis Leakey, and how they studied and reported on the behavior of three different primate species. Two things make this story fascinating. First, Leakey tended to encourage researchers who didn't have much scientific background. He was convinced that a lack of presuppositions made these three women better at observation. Second, all three women left quiet lives to become adventurers—living in jungles in faraway countries. The art is simple but excellent—especially the page layouts.

Reed, M. K., & Flood, J. (2016). *Science Comics: Dinosaurs: Fossils and Feathers.* First Second.
This graphic novel combines spellbinding art with detailed descriptions of dinosaurs' natural history, the mythology surrounding dinosaurs, how fossils happen, how dinosaurs were first discovered, the history of human interactions with dinosaur bones, a thorough discussion of dinosaur typology, and a discussion of the newest data and theories about dinosaurs. The data is strong, the presentation is interesting, and the art is spectacular. If you have ever had an interest, fascination, or borderline obsession with dinosaurs, this book is for you.

Telgemeier, R. (2019). *Guts.* Scholastic. While this is not exactly a science text, it tells the autobiographical story of Raina who has anxiety, and her anxiety causes digestive problems which cause more anxiety. The memoir tells the story of how she copes (and fails to cope) with an illness that is clearly connected both to her gut and her brain. This is a good book for connecting physiological ailments and symptoms with real human beings and understanding the toll that such diseases exact on real human lives.

VanderKlugt, K. (2020). *Science Comics: Crows: Genius Birds.* First Second. A crow frees Buddy, a dog, from his yard, then tutors him in all the ways to find food by using one's brain. Along the way, the crow explains about crow anatomy, capabilities, social interactions, family life, and more. This book is packed with information but embeds that knowledge in an interesting story about a crow teaching a dog and maybe getting the dog into trouble along the way. The illustrations are beautiful (most of the action takes place at the end of a day, and the sun is setting, allowing for beautiful sky and backgrounds), the story is interesting, and the information about crows is well-organized, well-researched, and teaches concepts as well as facts. This is the sort of book that left me thinking at the end that I didn't know how much I am interested in crows.

Viola, J. (2019). *Polar Bears: Survival on the Ice*. First Second. A mother polar bear and her two cubs allow us a glimpse into their lives in their graphic novel exploration of survival in the Arctic. As the mother polar bear teaches the cubs about which sorts of ice are strong enough to walk on, what it means to be a carnivore, how to stay cool, how to swim, how to catch seals, and all sorts of other vital knowledge to be a successful polar bear.

Wicks, M. (2015). *Human Body Theater*. First Second.
The conceit for this book is that the audience is attending a variety-show-style review in which each system of the body states center stage and describes for us how our body works. Chapters include the skeletal, muscular, respiratory, cardiovascular, digestive, excretory, endocrine, reproductive, and immune systems, as well as the senses. Wicks uses cartoonish depictions of the body parts in such a way that a disembodied heart or talking intestine does not seem a bit disgusting but somehow cute. The research here is up-to-date, solid, and emphasizes the ways body systems connect with each other. Expect some jokes and puns along the way. This is a fun and accurate way to learn about anatomy and health.

Wicks, M. (2016). *Science Comics: Coral Reefs: Cities of the Ocean*. First Second.
A bespectacled fish who lives in a coral reef explains the origins and biology of coral and describes the interdependent ecosystem that makes the coral reef its home. The book also explains how the coral reef ecosystem impacts the rest of the planet, and how the changes that humans are making on the planet are impacting coral reefs and their continued existence. Maris Wick's drawing style does a remarkable job of giving us a clear and accurate picture of what corals, sponges, sharks, octopi, phytoplankton, jellyfish, and the coral reef environment looks like. And yet at the same time, her realistic but cartoonish glasses-wearing fish and humans make the book one that is both accurate and also inviting. She forgoes giving us a weak libretto story that attempts to tie the information about the coral reef into some kind of overall narrative but instead makes the information she presents interesting through the image and the side comments she makes about the details. The result is a no-nonsense informative book that is a blast to read.

Willis, B. (2021). *Seen: Rachel Carson*. BOOM! Box. *Seen: Rachel Carson*, is part of a series of "True Stories of Marginalized Trailblazers." Rachel Carson's story covers her life as a biologist and writer who was influential in driving change in the United States and globally in the realm of environmental protection. Specifically, the book focuses on Rachel's work advocating for regulation and investigation of the effects of pesticides and herbicides on ecosystems.

Winick, J. (2000). *Pedro and Me: Friendship, Loss, and What I Learned.* Henry Holt and Company. *Pedro & Me* tells the story of the friendship between Pedro and Judd that began on the TV show The Real World. In addition to being HIV-positive, Pedro was an AIDS educator and during their six months of filming together became fast friends with Judd. This graphic novel tells the story of that friendship and the difficulty of walking alongside Pedro as he died from AIDS at twenty-two years old.

Woollcott, T. (2018). *The Brain: The Ultimate Thinking Machine.* First Second. Usually First Second's Science Comics series does a nice job of integrating the narrative story with the exposition. At times this one is not so smooth. The story is about a girl selling cookies who is captured by a mad scientist (who is actually a brain connected to a robot body) and his zombie assistant. While awaiting rescue, she must stop him from dissecting her brain by asking him questions about brains and how they work. The problem is not so much that the story is ridiculously cheesy (though it is), it is more than the subject of the book—the brain, has been cast as the villain but the hero, who is mostly focused on selling enough cookies to destroy her rivals, is not very likable either. While Nour is sometimes interested in what the mad scientist has to say, at other times, she is trying to escape and is ignoring what he is saying.

Physics

Brown, D. (2019). *Big Ideas That Changed The World: Rocket to the Moon.* Amulet Books. Covering over a century of history of rockets, the focus of the book is the space race between the United States and the USSR that culminated in the landing on the moon by Neil Armstrong and Buzz Aldrin on Apollo 11 in July 1969. The GN offers an authentic account, including numerous failures along the way that preceded the eventual success. A timeline of the twentieth century at the end of the book helps the reader to situation the moon mission within a larger context that now includes MIR and the International Space Station as well as more recent initiatives by SPACEX.

Cunningham, D. (2017). *Graphic Science: Seven Journeys of Discovery.* Oxford: Myriad. *Graphic Science* presents biographies of chemist Antoine Lavoisier, proto-paleontologist Mary Anning, botanist George Washington Carver, physicist and engineer Nikola Tesla, geological theorist Alfred Wegener, physicist Jocelyn Bell Burnell, and astronomer Fred Hoyle. The idea here is to show how science developed over 200 years by focusing on these seven lives. The books show them in their social, cultural, and political contexts to highlight the way science contends with societal response to theories and discoveries. It is a fairly good graphic novel, though it does not make as much use of moment-to-moment transitions as it might and sometimes seems to function more like an illustrated picture book, just with lots of panels. The light this book shines on the lives of scientists with whom many students might not be familiar is admirable. Having said all that, it is a fascinating book and well worth a read.

Drozd, A., & Drozd, J. (2018). *Rockets: Defying Gravity.* First Second. This GN summarizes the evolution of rockets and the overarching physics (classical mechanics, escape velocity, etc.). There are detailed drawings and illustrative examples to describe the physics underlying rocket design. The GN traces the historical development of the automobile from 400 BCE through the space race until the modern era (private rocket companies, e.g., SpaceX).

Einhorn, H., Staffaroni, A., & Harvey, J. (2021). *The Curie Society.* The MIT Press. Three new students at Edmonds University receive a secret code leading to an invitation to join the Curie Society. Through collaboration and application of their unique expertise, they help leaders of this group to foil an evil plot. The book does an excellent job of demonstrating growth mindset (e.g., learning through making mistakes) and the power of collaboration. It is also a really exciting book that will grab the attention of upper elementary and middle school students especially.

Fetter-Vorm, J. (2019). *Moonbound: Apollo 11 and the Dream of Spaceflight.* Hill and Wang. The story of humans' first journey to the face of the moon has got to be one of the most exciting and compelling stories of the modern world. This focused graphic novel describes the Apollo project, and how NASA gathered a team of astronauts, engineers, and specialists, and together they did trial runs and eventually took off from Earth, landed on the moon, and got back. The realistic images, sense of drama, and excellent connections of words and images in this book make it a gripping tale. They came close to disaster on more than one occasion. There are a lot of valuable descriptions of engineering, physics, and history here too.

Kirshbaum, J. (2019). *Skyscrapers: The Heights of Engineering.* First Second. A superhero who looks remarkably similar to another guy with a cape and an S on his chest, along with his sidekick Quiz Kid, finds out about the history, engineering, and design of skyscrapers by literally running into them during patrols of the city and going back in time to look at the design elements of the pyramids, medieval cathedrals, and the first real skyscrapers. Along the way the reader learns about the forces of gravity, compression, wind shear, and other aspects of physics that are part of designing a skyscraper.

Latta, S. (2017). *Smash!*. Graphic Universe. This graphic novel describes the building blocks of quarks, the work of the Large Hadron Collider at CERN, and other concepts like dark energy, the effect of gravity, and dark matter. The broader story depicts two cousins visiting CERN and learning about the history and background of particle physics.

Mosco, R. (2018). *Solar System: Our Place in Space*. First Second. Sara is homesick and is bored. Her friend Jill is trying to find ways to entertain her and finally hits upon the idea of using her book about the planets to make up a story for Sara in which their pets become the intrepid crew of an exploration spaceship. The ship runs on Sara's interest level, which is pretty low at first, but as they check out new planets, her interest level rises and so does the ship's energy stores. As they explore each planet we find out everything from orbits and gravity to moons and atmosphere composition. It is a nicely put-together book.

Nitta, H., Yakamoto, M., & Takatsu, K. (2011). *The Manga Guide to Relativity*. No Starch Press, Inc. This *Manga Guide* explores the topic of relativity through the eyes of the traditional Manga characters. From introductory discussions of Newtonian Mechanics, this graphic novel provides an engaging and visual presentation of familiar topics from the first-year physics curriculum, including the speed of light, the Urishima Effect (time dilation), Lorentz Contraction, gravity, and general relativity. Extensions and applications such as black holes and global position systems (GPS) are provided near the end of this graphic novel. Students taking a first course in physics will connect with the interactive and engaging presentation of the scientific terms. Detailed diagrams and images are interpreted by the Manga characters in ways that high school and university students will understand. Like many other *Manga Guides*, this graphic novel is an excellent resource for teachers and students.

Ottaviani, J., Cannon, Z., & Cannon, K. (2009). *T-Minus: The Race to the Moon*. Aladdin. This book shows both the US and USSR sides of the space race. We see engineers, mathematicians, and scientists working together to theorize, design, and build a system for getting humans to the moon. The book emphasizes cooperation (including at least some sharing between engineers on both sides of the iron curtain, and industry putting the mission before profits). It is also simply an exciting and gripping true-life story. The math, engineering, and physics in this graphic novel are interesting, but it is the exciting story and its potential to win over reluctant students that have the most potential in this book.

Ottaviani, J., Barr, D., & Gladden, S. (1998). *Dignifying Science: Stories about Women Scientists*. G.T. Labs. This book is an excellent series of biographies of women who made a huge difference in science including

Hedy Lamarr, Lise Mietner, Rosalind Franklin, Barbara McClintlock, and Biruté Galdikas. The stories are not only scientifically important but also interesting to read, covering everything from the science of spying to the science of discovering atomic structure.

Ottaviani, J., Johnston, J., Lieber, S., Parker, J., Mireault, B., & Kemple, C. (2001). *Fallout: J Robert Oppenhiemer, Leo Szilard, and the Political Science of the Atomic Bomb.* G.T. Labs. The story of how mathematicians and physicists got together and built the most powerful weapon ever known is endlessly fascinating. This book looks at the life of Oppenheimer, who tried to direct and corral the scientists and military advisers and somehow managed to move the project forward in spite of personality conflicts and conflicting ideologies. Much of this story will be familiar to many readers, but not the latter part of the book, which concerns Oppenheimer's trial under McCarthyism and his subsequent loss of a post with the Atomic Energy Commission because he had been part of a group with communist connections when he was a young student. There is a lot of good stuff in here about how scientists and the government interact.

Ottaviani, J., & Myrick, L. (2013). *Feynman.* First Second. Richard Feynman is famous as one of the most prolific physicists of the modern era, helping to develop the atomic bomb, winning the Nobel Prize, and developing some of the most influential lectures for physics ever. This GN provides a biography of Feynman, including scenes from his childhood and personal life as well as a detailed focus of his time at Los Alamos, MIT, Cornell, and Caltech. This book closely follows similar narratives to Feynman's popular autobiography, *Surely You're Joking Mr. Feynman* (1985), but has detailed explanations and illustrations in the back half of the Feynman lectures and the Alix Mautner Lectures, which are arguably some of the most approachable and understandable explanations of quantum physics ever developed.

Ottaviani, J., & Myrick, L. (2019). *Hawking.* First Second. This graphic novel biography follows astrophysicist Stephen Hawking from his youth, through college and grad school, and his rise to a position of prominence as one of the most respected scientists of our age. It also follows the progression of ALS, a degenerative neuromuscular disease as it took away his ability to walk, speak clearly, and eventually nearly everything, except his ability to think. It also follows Stephen's relationship with his wife and children, his divorce from his wife, and his remarriage. All three strands are woven together in a well-balanced. well-written, and masterfully illustrated narrative that will give the reader plenty to think about.

Ottaviani, J., & Purvis, L. (2009). *Suspended in Language.* G.T. Labs. This graphic novel gives a biographical summary of Niels Bohr's life. Starting with his work on surface tension, through the award-winning Bohr model of the atom, until his contributions to the Copenhagen interpretation of quantum mechanics, and finally ending with the founding of CERN. The book is heavy on anecdotes about Bohr's life, particularly in the first half, and points out Bohr's eccentric ways of communicating at many points.

Ottaviani, J., & Wicks, M. (2020). *Astronauts: Women on the Final Frontier.* First Second. *Astronauts* follows the story of Mary Cleave, one of the first female astronauts in NASA. It details the history of many of the first female astronauts and cosmonauts and goes through, in detail, the requirements and achievements during the space shuttle program. The graphic novel gives a detailed account of the highly competitive field of becoming an astronaut, and the glamorous and unglamorous elements of going into space.

Seagle, S. T., & Kristiansen, T. (2013). *Genius.* First Second. Ted is a physicist near the midpoint of his career. His job is in jeopardy unless he can come through with a breakthrough in his research soon. When he finds out that his senile father-in-law worked as a military policeman and that Albert Einstein confided in him about some ideas he was working on, Ted sees a solution. All he has to do is get the information out of his hostile and incoherent father-in-law. Somewhere along the way, though, Ted begins to ask himself what it is he wants out of life.

Tatsuta, K. (2017). *Ichi-F: A Worker's Graphic Memoir of the Fukushima Nuclear Power.* Kodansha Comics. The graphic novel provides an overview of the cleanup of the nuclear power plants after the Fukushima disaster. Focus is given to the mundane tasks that labor workers undergo, including the use of protective equipment and the monitoring of radiation dosages.

Wilgus, B. (2017). *Flying Machines: How the Wright Brothers Soared.* First Second. Narrated by the younger sister of the Wright brothers, this graphic novel describes the problems and challenges the Wrights and other inventors faced in making a working flying machine. Along the way readers learn history, aerodynamics, engineering, and general science.

Technology

Brown, B. (2016). *Tetris: The Games People Play.* First Second. Brown dives into the history of the well-known game by following its creator, Alexey Pajitnov, who worked as a computer scientist for the Soviet government. With iconic yellow, white, and black illustrations, this graphic novel talks about a bit of the history of game development, including arcade cabinet games through to the Gameboy, and the politics of releasing it to the world.

Einhorn, H., Staffaroni, A., & Harvey, J. (2021). *The Curie Society.* The MIT Press. Three new students at Edmonds University receive a secret code leading to an invitation to join the Curie Society. Through collaboration and application of their unique expertise, they help leaders of this group to foil an evil plot. The book does an excellent job of demonstrating growth mindset (e.g., learning through making mistakes) and the power of collaboration. It is also a really exciting book that will grab the attention of upper elementary and middle school students especially.

Fetter-Vorm, J. (2019). *Moonbound: Apollo 11 and the Dream of Spaceflight.* Hill and Wang. The story of humans' first journey to the face of the moon is one of the most exciting and compelling stories of the modern world. This focused graphic novel describes the Apollo project, and how NASA gathered a team of astronauts, engineers, and specialists, and together they did trial runs and eventually took off from Earth, landed on the moon, and got back. The realistic images, sense of drama, and excellent connections of words and images in this book make it a gripping tale. They came close to disaster on more than one occasion. There are a lot of valuable descriptions of engineering, physics, and history here too.

Ottaviani, J., Cannon, Z., & Cannon, K. (2009). *T-Minus: The Race to the Moon.* Aladdin. This book shows both the US and USSR sides of the space race. We see engineers, mathematicians, and scientists working together to theorize, design, and build a system for getting humans to the moon. The book emphasizes cooperation (including at least some sharing between engineers on both sides of the iron curtain, and industry putting the mission before profits). It is also simply an exciting and gripping true-life story. The math, engineering, and physics in this graphic novel are interesting, but it is the exciting story and its potential to win over reluctant students that have the most potential in this book.

Ottaviani, J., & Purvis, L. (2016). *The Imitation Game: Alan Turing Decoded.* Harry N. Abrams. Alan Turing is famous for his role in helping the Allies break the code of the German's Enigma machine during the Second World War. This GN provides a biography of Turing, including scenes from his childhood and education as well as a detailed focus of his time at Bletchley Park during the war and his subsequent work in computer science. Some readers may be familiar with a movie by the same title, and the GN provides a richer account of this complicated person's life.

Padua, S. (2015). *The Thrilling Adventures of Lovelace and Babbage.* Penguin. Ada Byron Lovelace meets Charles Babbage. Babbage has designed (but not built) a machine called the Difference Engine, which is essentially the first clearly envisioned plan for a kind of computer. Lovelace meets Babbage, has an excited, largely mathematical conversation with him, and soon is writing imaginary computer programs for the Difference Engine—the first real computer programs ever written. And just as the story is getting exciting and you are thinking that the Difference Engine will allow Britain to jump to the lead of the Industrial Revolution, Lovelace dies young and Babbage fails to get the Difference Engine built. So the creator of this graphic novel, Sydney Padua, then imagines a pocket universe in which Lovelace did not die early and she and Babbage built the Difference Engine and made it available to serve the Queen. What follows is a delightfully imagined silly story. If you love weird history, interesting theoretical math, or strange fiction, this book is for you. It is creatively imagined, delightfully rendered, and a lot of fun to read—if it fits your sense of humor. The footnotes alone are hilarious.

Schweizer, C. (2019). *Maker Comics: Fix a Car.* First Second. Ms. Gritt runs a Saturday morning car maintenance club. The members of the club include Abner, who is an old street racer; Lena, who drives a truck; Rocky and Esther, who are two middle school kids who are really interested in engineering; and Mason, who drives an old sedan. Over the course of the book, Ms Gritt teaches them everything from checking the fluid levels to replacing the drive belt.

Scott, M. (2018). *Robots and Drones: Past, Present, and Future.* First Second. With Archytas's robot bird as our guide, this book explores the history of the development of robots by trying to define what a robot is. Maybe that doesn't sound so exciting, but it is the amazing details about what robots can do, how they are made, and how they accomplish what they accomplish that makes this a fascinating book.

Shibuya, M., Takashi, T., & Sawa, O. (2017). *The Manga Guide to Microprocessors.* No Starch Press, Inc. This is another in the growing series of *Manga Guides* graphic novels. Any student taking a first course in computer science would welcome the opportunity to explore concepts in this format that develops meaning through images and text. Topics such as the central processing unit (CPU), binary arithmetic, logical gates and operations, circuits, memory types and devices, assembly and high-level programs, and microcontrollers are introduced through the eyes and experiences of the *Manga* characters. While this book would probably not be an ideal first for first-year computer programming courses, it might be an ideal exploration for high school students wishing to explore aspects of computer science as a discipline.

Yang, G. L., & Holmes, M. (2015). *Secret Coders.* First Second. Hopper is a new girl at Stately Academy. Though she has trouble fitting in, she is more troubled by the angry janitor who yells at her and the creepy birds that seem to be staring at her. When she finally finds a friend, Eni, and then she finds a robot in the janitor's shed and at the same time, she also finds a mystery. One that will require math and logic to solve.

Yang, G. L., & Holmes, M. (2018). *Secret Coders: Monsters and Modules.* First Second. Hopper, Eni, and Josh have opened the portal into Flatland. Now all they need to do is go through it, rescue the second Turtle of Light, bring it back with them, and defeat Dr. One-Zero before he can enslave the world—and before their parents break up the group. This book wraps up the series in a satisfying way.

Yang, G. L., & Holmes, M. (2016). *Secret Coders: Paths and Portals.* First Second. The coders are back. Hopper, Eni, and Josh now discover that Mr. Bee, the grumpy janitor from the first book, was once a teacher at the school, and he begins to teach them while at the same time, they begin to dig into some of the suspicious doings that the dean of the school (and his pet rugby team) seem involved in. When the dean captures one of the janitor's robots, and then the janitor himself, the secret coders need to decide if it is worth unleashing chaos to set the janitor free.

Yang, G. L., & Holmes, M. (2018). *Secret Coders: Potions and Parameters.* First Second. The secret coders have their hands full this time. The evil Dr. One-Zero not only has managed to put together enough of his Green Pop formula to enslave the world, but worse, he has control of the Turtle of Light. Professor Bea explains that their only hope is if Hopper, Eni, and Josh can figure out how to use their coding skills to open a portal into another dimension.

Yang, G. L., & Homes, M. (2017). *Secret Coders: Robots and Repeats.* First Second. Hopper, Eni, and Josh, the secret coders, have found their mentor, Professor Bea, hiding in an underground complex. While he continues to teach them in secret, they also must attend the classes taught by Dr. One-Zero who is using the students of their school to manufacture his Green Pop which leaves people mindless. So again the coders must save the city, and again it is their coding abilities, along with the amazing Turtle of Light that must win the day.

Yang, G. L., & Holmes, M. (2017). *Secret Coders: Secrets and Sequences.* First Second. As in earlier adventures, Hopper, Eni, and Josh, the secret coders, must work collaboratively to overcome challenges posed by Dr. One-Zero. After learning about writing procedures with a parameter to draw triangles of varying sizes, the programming heroes create parameter-based procedures that can be modified to have the turtle trace out the exact regular hexagon which functions as a path portal. These graphic novels, like the others in the series, highlight the intersection of geometric reasoning, Logo programming, and problem-solving.

Zettwoch, D. (2019). *Cars: Engines That Move You.* First Second. The GN traces the historical development of the automobile from the mid-1800s through the time of Henry Ford (assembly lines, "tin lizzie") and culminating with alternative fuel vehicles of the early twenty-first century (electric, hybrid, etc.). Rather than a novel structure, this GN is an amalgamation of images and descriptions that reads more like an encyclopedia than a compelling story.

Engineering

Drozd, A., & Drozd, J. (2018). *Rockets: Defying Gravity.* First Second. This GN summarizes the evolution of rockets and the overarching physics (classical mechanics, escape velocity, etc.). There are detailed drawings and illustrative examples to describe the physics underlying rocket design. The GN traces the historical development of the automobile from 400 BCE through the space race until the modern era (private rocket companies, e.g., SpaceX).

Brown, D. (2019). *Big Ideas That Changed The World: Rocket to the Moon.* Amulet Books. Covering over a century of history of rockets, the focus of the book is the space race between the United States and the USSR that culminated in the landing on the moon by Neil Armstrong and Buzz Aldrin on Apollo 11 in July 1969. The GN offers an authentic account, including numerous failures along the way that preceded the eventual success. A timeline of the twentieth century at the end of the book helps the reader to situation the moon mission within a larger context that now includes MIR and the International Space Station as well as more recent initiatives by SpaceX.

Fetter-Vorm, J. (2019). *Moonbound: Apollo 11 and the Dream of Spaceflight.* Hill and Wang. The story of humans' first journey to the face of the moon has got to be one of the most exciting and compelling stories of the modern world. This focused graphic novel describes the Apollo project, and how NASA gathered a team of astronauts, engineers, and specialists, and together they did trial runs and eventually took off from Earth, landed on the moon, and got back. The realistic images, sense of drama, and excellent connections of words and images in this book makes it a gripping tale. They came close to disaster on more than one occasion. There are a lot of valuable descriptions of engineering, physics, and history here too.

Kerschbaum, J. (2019). *Skyscrapers: The Heights of Engineering.* First Second. A superhero who looks remarkably similar to another guy with a cape and an S on his chest, along with his sidekick Quiz Kid, finds out of about the history, engineering, and design of skyscrapers by literally running into them during patrols of the city and going back in time to look at the design elements of the pyramids, medieval cathedrals, and the first real skyscrapers. Along the way the reader learns about the forces of gravity, compression, wind shear, and other aspects of physics that are part of designing a skyscraper.

Ottaviani, J., Cannon, Z., & Cannon, K. (2009). *T-Minus: The Race to the Moon*. Aladdin. This book shows both the US and USSR sides of the space race. We see engineers, mathematicians, and scientists working together to theorize, design, and build a system for getting humans to the moon. The book emphasizes cooperation (including at least some sharing between engineers on both sides of the iron curtain, and industry putting the mission before profits). It is also simply an exciting and gripping true-life story. The math, engineering, and physics in this graphic novel are interesting, but it is the exciting story and its potential to win over reluctant students that have the most potential in this book.

Ottaviani, J., & Wicks, M. (2020). *Astronauts: Women on the Final Frontier*. First Second. *Astronauts* follows the story of Mary Cleave, one of the first female astronauts in NASA. It details the history of many of the first female astronauts and cosmonauts and goes through, in detail, the requirements and achievements during the space shuttle program. The graphic novel gives a detailed account of the highly competitive field of becoming an astronaut, and the glamorous and unglamorous elements of going into space.

Schweitzer, C. (2019). *Maker Comics: Fix a Car*. First Second.
Ms. Gritt runs a Saturday morning car maintenance club. The members of the club include Abner, who is an old street racer; Lena, who drives a truck; Rocky and Esther, who are two middle school kids who are really interested in engineering; and Mason, who drives an old sedan. Over the course of the book, Ms Gritt teaches them everything from checking the fluid levels to replacing the drive belt. Along the way, we get to know each of the members of the club and it is honestly interesting to see the story unwind. We expected the narrative story to seem like a contrivance all the way through, but it was a real story that also teaches readers real important information. The art is excellent in that it gives us insights into what the students are thinking, but also shows each mechanical operation with great detail.

Scott, M. (2018). *Robots and Drones: Past, Present, and Future*. First Second. With Archytas's robot bird as our guide, this book explores the history of the development of robots by trying to define what a robot is. Maybe that doesn't sound so exciting, but it is the amazing details about what robots can do, how they are made, and how they accomplish what they accomplish that makes this a fascinating book

Tatsuta, K. (2017). *Ichi-F: A Worker's Graphic Memoir of the Fukushima Nuclear Power*. Kodansha Comics. The graphic novel provides an overview of the cleanup of the nuclear power plants after the Fukushima disaster. Focus is given to the mundane tasks that labor workers undergo, including the use of protective equipment and the monitoring of radiation dosages.

Tomasi, P. (2018). *The Bridge*. Harry N. Abrams. The bridge tells the story of Colonel Washington Roebling in building the Brooklyn Bridge across the east river in New York. The bridge project overcame significant obstacles, being one of the most ambitious construction projects of its time, was mired in physical, political, and social obstacles, and is an inspirational story demonstrating the hardships and difficult choices that were made by civil engineers.

Wilgus, B. (2017). *Flying Machines: How the Wright Brothers Soared*. First Second. Narrated by the little sister of the Wright brothers, this graphic novel describes the problems and challenges the Wrights and other inventors faced in making a working flying machine. Along the way readers learn history, aerodynamics, engineering, and general science.

Zettwoch, D. (2019). *Cars: Engines That Move You*. First Second. The GN traces the historical development of the automobile from the mid-1800s through the time of Henry Ford (assembly lines, "tin lizzie") and culminating with alternative fuel vehicles of the early twenty-first century (electric, hybrid, etc.). Rather than a novel structure, this GN is an amalgamation of images and descriptions that reads more like an encyclopedia than a compelling story.

Mathematics

Andriopoulos, T. (2010). *Who Killed Professor X?*. Birkhauser. Shortly after giving the opening lecture of a worldwide math conference, a famous German mathematician, called Professor X, (no relation to the X-Men's mentor) falls over dead in a hotel dining room. A police inspector is called in and, with the help of a trusted mathematician, begins to try to determine who committed the crime. One of the difficulties, however, is that the suspects are mathematicians and have given statements that are full of math language. So the inspector and his assistant must solve the problems to determine the location of each suspect at the moment of the murder. As the inspector goes through each of the suspects, his assistant, Kurt, fills us in on their backgrounds. The suspects include some familiar names: Rene, Blaise, Isaac, Leonhard, Carl Friedrich, Pheidias, and Sophie. We learn about them and their lives as we consider whether they might have been the murderer. Working on the solution provides another piece of the puzzle necessary for solving the mystery.

Doxiadis, A., Papadimitriou, Christos H., Papadatos, A., & DiDonna, A. (2009). *Logicomix: An Epic Search for Truth*. Bloomsbury. This excellent story follows the life of Bertrand Russell and his attempt to discover truth through mathematics, philosophy, and physics. Good explanations of geometry, paradox, infinity, and the difference between computation and higher math—with a fair amount of secrecy, scandal, madness, and mystery mixed in.

Klein, G., & Dabney, A. (2013). *The Cartoon Introduction to Statistics*. Hill and Wang. Follow the adventures of a variety of characters as they first explore the process of gathering data, highlighting the difference between random and convenience samples. Next, the characters describe numerical data with visual displays, exploring different shapes for sample distributions. Later, measures of central tendency ("averages") and dispersion ("spread") are illustrated with practical examples. The second half of the book starts with an exploration of the Central Limit Theorem, proceeds to hypothesis testing and confidence intervals, and finishes with some cautions regarding the interpretation of statistical results. While this is not a statistics textbook, it would make an excellent auxiliary resource for teachers and students alike. This graphic novel would be helpful for any student of statistics, including at the middle school, high school, and university levels.

Ottaviani, J., Cannon, Z., & Cannon, K. (2009). *T-Minus: The Race to the Moon*. Aladdin. This book shows both the US and USSR sides of the space race. We see engineers, mathematicians, and scientists working together to theorize, design, and build a system for getting humans to the moon. The book emphasizes cooperation (including at least some sharing between engineers on both sides of the iron curtain, and industry putting the mission before profits). It is also simply an exciting and gripping true-life story. The math, engineering, and physics in this graphic novel are interesting, but it is the exciting story and its potential to win over reluctant students that have the most potential in this book.

Ottaviani, J., & Purvis, L. (2016). *The Imitation Game: Alan Turing Decoded*. Harry N. Abrams. Alan Turing is famous for his role in helping the Allies break the code of the German's Enigma machine during the Second World War. This GN provides a biography of Turing, including scenes from his childhood and education as well as a detailed focus of his time at Bletchley Park during the war and his subsequent work in computer science. Some readers may be familiar with a movie by the same title, and the GN provides a richer account of this complicated person's life.

Yang, G. L., & Holmes, M. (2016). *Secret Coders: Paths and Portals*. First Second. The coders are back. Hopper, Eni, and Josh now discover that Mr. Bee, the grumpy janitor from the first book, was once a teacher at the school, and he begins to teach them while at the same time, they begin to dig into some of the suspicious doings that the dean of the school (and his pet rugby team) seem involved in. When the dean captures one of the janitor's robots, and then the janitor himself, the secret coders need to decide if it is worth unleashing chaos to set the janitor free.

Yang, G. L., & Holmes, M. (2015). *Secret Coders*. First Second. Hopper is a new girl at Stately Academy. Though she has trouble fitting in, she is more troubled by the angry janitor who yells at her and the creepy birds that seem to be staring at her. When she finally finds a friend, Eni, and then she finds a robot in the janitor's shed, and at the same time, she also finds a mystery. One that will require math and logic to solve.

Yang, G. L., & Holmes, M. (2018). *Secret Coders: Monsters and Modules*. First Second. Hopper, Eni, and Josh have opened the portal into Flatland. Now all they need to do is go through it, rescue the second Turtle of Light, bring it back with them, and defeat Dr. One-Zero before he can enslave the world—and before their parents break up the group. This book wraps up the series in a satisfying way.

Yang, G. L., & Holmes, M. (2018). *Secret Coders: Potions and Parameters*. First Second. The secret coders have their hands full this time. The evil Dr. One-Zero not only has managed to put together enough of his Green Pop formula to enslave the world, but worse, he has control of the Turtle of Light. Professor Bea explains that their only hope is if Hopper, Eni, and Josh can figure out how to use their coding skills to open a portal into another dimension.

Yang, G. L., & Holmes, M. (2017). *Secret Coders: Robots and Repeats*. First Second. Hopper, Eni, and Josh, the secret coders, have found their mentor, Professor Bea, hiding in an underground complex. While he continues to teach them in secret, they also must attend the classes taught by Dr. One-Zero who is using the students of their school to manufacture his Green Pop which leaves people mindless. So again the coders must save the city, and again it is their coding abilities, along with the amazing Turtle of Light that must win the day.

Yang, G. L., & Holmes, M. (2017). *Secret Coders: Secrets and Sequences*. First Second. As in earlier adventures, Hopper, Eni, and Josh, the secret coders, must work collaboratively to overcome challenges posed by Dr. One-Zero. After learning about writing procedures with a parameter to draw triangles of varying sizes, the programming heroes create parameter-based procedures that can be modified to have the turtle trace out the exact regular hexagon which functions as a path portal. This graphic novel, like the others in the series, highlights the intersection of geometric reasoning, Logo programming, and problem-solving.

Yang, G. L., & Kim, D. K. (2010). *Prime Baby*. First Second. A middle school student named Thaddeus has difficulty understanding his baby sister Maddie. After learning about prime numbers in school and their potential use by NASA scientists as a universal language for communicating with alien lifeforms, Thaddeus decides to decode the apparent ramblings of his baby sister. To his amazement, he documents that Maddie's speech patterns appear to follow the sequence of prime numbers from 2 to 19. Readers of this graphic novel are introduced to the first eight prime numbers, and this might be useful in the initial exploration of this mathematical concept.

WORKS CITED

Abadzis, N. (2007). *Laika*. New York: First Second.

Abbott, E. A. (1884). *Flatland: A Romance of Many Dimensions*. London: Seeley & Co.

Akbar, A. P. (2019). *Using English Comic Strips to Help Senior High School Students Write Narrative Text and Improve Their Writing Achievement* (Masters Thesis). Jember University.

Albright, K. S., & Gavigan, K. (2014). Information Vaccine: Using Graphic Novels as an HIV/AIDS Prevention Resource for Young Adults. *Journal of Education for Library and Information Science*, 55(2), 178–85.

Aldahash, R., & Altahab, S. (2020). The Effect of Graphic Novels on EFL Learners Comprehension. *Journal of Applied Linguistics and English Literature*, 9(5), 19–26.

Andriopoulos, T., & Gkiokas, T. (2015). *Who Killed Professor X?* London: Birkhauser.

Aoi, S., Tanaka, T., Fujiki, S., Funato, T., Senda, K., & Tsuchiya, K. (2016). Advantage of Straight Walk Instability in Turning Maneuver of Multilegged Locomotion: A Robotics Approach. *Scientific Reports*, 6, 30199. https://doi.org/10.1038/srep30199

Armstrong, P. (2016). *Bloom's Taxonomy*. Nashville: Vanderbilt University Center for Teaching.

Arnett, D. (2008). Implementing Graphic Novels into the Language Arts Classroom. *Minnesota English Journal*, 44(1), 150–79.

Auerbach, A., & Codor, R. (2017). *Max the Demon vs. Entropy of Doom: The Epic Mission of Maxwell's Demon to Face the 2nd Law of Thermodynamics and Save Earth from Environmental Disaster*. Brooklyn: Loose Line Productions.

Boerman-Cornell, W. (2013). Exploring the Text/Image Wilderness: Ironic Visual Perspective and Critical Thinking in George O'Connor's Graphic Novel. *Journey into Mohawk Country. Bookbird: A Journal of International Children's Literature*, 51(4), 29–34.

Boerman-Cornell, W. (2015). Using Historical Graphic Novels in High School History Classes: Potential for Contextualization, Sourcing, and Corroborating. *The History Teacher*, 48(2), 209–24.

Boerman-Cornell, W., & Kim, J. (2020). *Using Graphic Novels in the English Language Arts Classroom*. London: Bloomsbury Academic.

Boerman-Cornell, W., Kim, J., & Manderino, M. L. (2017). *Graphic Novels in High School and Middle School Classrooms*. Lanham: Rowman and Littlefield.

Boerman-Cornell, W., Klanderman, D., & Schut, A. (2017). Using Harry Potter to Bridge Higher Dimensionality in Mathematics and High-Interest Literature. *Journal of Adolescent & Adult Literacy*, 60(4), 425–32.

Bransford, John D., & Donovan, S. (2005). *How Students Learn: History, Mathematics, and Science in the Classroom*. Washington D.C.: The National Academies Press.

Brooks, Rodney A., & Flynn, A. (1989). Fast, Cheap, and Out of Control: A Robot Invasion of the Solar System. *Journal of the British Interplanetary Society, 42*, 478–85.

Brown, B. (2016). *Tetris: The Games People Play*. New York: First Second.

Brown, D. (2019). *Rocket to the Moon: Big Ideas that Changed the World*. New York: Amulet Books.

Brozo, W. G. (2015). Would you Mortgage your DNA?: Prompting Meaningful Reading and Writing in Science with Genome. *Voices from the Middle, 22*(3), 19–23.

Brozo, W. G., & Mayville, M. (2012). Reforming Secondary Disciplinary Instruction with Graphic Novels. *The NERA Journal, 48*(1), 11–20.

Chad, J. (2016). *Science Comics: Volcanoes: Fire and Life*. New York: First Second.

Chun, C. (2009). Critical Literacies and Graphic Novels for English Language Learners: Teaching Maus. *Journal of Adolescent and Adult Literacy, 53*(2), 144–5.

Conners, S. P. (2010). *Multimodal Reading: A Case Study of High School Students in an After-School Graphic Novel Reading Group* (Doctoral Dissertation). Proquest.

Conners, S. P. (2012). Weaving Multimodal Meaning in a Graphic Novel Reading Group. *Visual Communication, 12*: 27–53.

Cook, M. (2014). *Reading Graphically: Examining the Effects of Graphic Novels on the Reading Comprehension of High School Students* (Dissertation). Proquest.

Cunningham, D. (2017). *Graphic Science: Seven Journeys of Discovery*. Oxford: Myriad.

Cunningham, D., & Revkin, A. C. (2013). *How to Fake a Moon Landing: Exposing the Myths of Science Denial*. New York: Harry Abrams.

Czerwiec, M. K., Williams, I., Squier, S. M., Green, Michael J., Myers Kimberly, R., & Smith, S. T. (2015). *Graphic Medicine Manifesto*. University Park: Pennsylvania State University Press.

Darraugh, L. (2018). Loving and Loathing: Portrayals of School Mathematics in Young Adult Fiction. *Journal for Research in Mathematics Education, 49*(2), 178–209.

Davis, L., Hilario, M., & Longia, K. (2019). *Debian Perl: Digital Detective Book 1*. Portland: Oni Press.

DeGracia, A. (2012). Images and Limited Text in Narrative: Using David Small's NonFiction Graphic Novel *Stitches* to Teach Memoir. *The ALAN Review, 40*(1), 56–63.

Doxiadis, A., Papadimitriou, C., Papadatos, A., & Di Donna, A. (2009). *Logicomix*. New York: Bloomsbury.

Drozd, A., & Drozd, J. (2018). *Science Comics: Rockets Defying Gravity*. New York: First Second.

Engineerscanada.ca, engineerscanada.ca/publications/public-guidelines-on-the-code -of-ethics. Accessed September 8, 2022.

Fetter-Vorm, J. (2012). *Trinity: A Graphic History of the First Atomic Bomb*. New York: Macmillan.

Fetter-Vorm, J. (2013). *Trinity: A Graphic History of the First Atomic Bomb*. New York: Hill and Wang.

Feynman, R. P. (1985). *Surely You're Joking, Mr. Feynman: Adventures of a Curious Character*. New York: W.W. Norton.

Fleshman, A. (2018). Engaging Students in Quantum Theory Using a Graphic Novel about Niels Bohr. In C. M. Teague & D. E. Gardner, *Engaging Students in Physical Chemistry* (pp. 183–201). Washington D.C.: American Chemical Society.

Frey, N., & Fisher, D. (2004). Using Graphic Novels, Anime, and the Internet in an Urban High School. *The English Journal, 93*(3), 19–25.

Gavigan, K. (2011). More Powerful than a Locomotive: Using Graphic Novels to Motivate Male Adolescent Readers. *Journal of Research on Libraries and Young Adults, 3*. https://www.yalsa.ala.org/jrlya/2011/06/more-powerful-than-a-locomotive-using-graphic-novels-to-motivate-struggling-male-adolescent-readers/.

Gavigan, K. W. (2010). *Examining Struggling Male Adolescent Readers' Responses to Graphic Novels: A Multiple Case Study of Four Eighth-Grade males In a Graphic Novel Book Club* (Dissertation). University of North Carolina Greensboro.

Gillenwater, C. (2014). Reading Images: The Phenomenon of Intertextuality and How it May Contribute to Developing Visual Literacy with Advanced Placement English Language Arts Students. *Journal of Ethnographic and Qualitative Research, 8*(4), n.p.

Gomes, C., & Carter, J. B. (2010). Navigating Through Social Norms, Negotiating Place: How *American Born Chinese* Motivates Struggling Readers. *English Journal, 100*(2), 68–76.

Greenberg, I., Patterson, E., & Canlas, J. (2020). *The Machine Never Blinks*. Seattle: Fantagraphics Books.

Groenke, S., & Savitz, R. (2016). "Smarter Than We Give Them Credit For"? Assumptions and Disruptions in a Summer Reading Program. *Voices from the Middle*, 24(2): 28–31.

Hale, N. (2018). *One Trick Pony*. New York: Harry Abrams.

Hammond, H. (2011). Graphic Novels and Multiliteracy: A High School Study with American Born Chinese. *Bookbird*, 50(4), 22–32.

Hammond, H. K. (2009). *Graphic Novels and Multimodal Literacy: A Reader-Response Study* (Ph.D. Dissertation). University of Minnesota.

Hirsch, A. (2019). *Science Comics: Cats: Nature and Nurture*. New York: First Second.

Ho, J., Klanderman, D., Klanderman, S., & Turner, J. (2023). Using Graphic Novels in the Teaching and Learning of Mathematics and Physics. *ACMS Journal and Proceeding* (Vol. 23, pp. 143–55). Wheaton: Association of Christians in the Mathematical Sciences.

Hosler, J. (1998). *Clan Apis*. Columbus: Active Synapse.

Hosler, J. (2021). *The Way of the Hive: A Honey Bee's Story*. New York: Harper Alley.

Hosler, J. (2015). *Last of the Sandwalkers*. New York: First Second.

Howard, A. (2017). *Dinosaur Empire: Journey through the Mesozoic Era*. New York: Harry Abrams.

Hughes, J., & Morrison, L. (2014). The Evolution of Teaching with Gra[hic Novels. *Jeunesse: Young People, Texts, Culture, 6*(2), 116–27.

Hughes, J. M., King, A., Perkins, P., & Fuke, V. (2011). Adolescents and "Autographics": Reading and Writing Coming-of-Age Graphic Novels. *Journal of Adolescent and Adult Literacy, 54*(8), 601–12.

Jee, B. D., & Anggoro, F. K. (2012). Comic Cognition: Exploring the Potential Cognitive Impacts of Science Comics. *Journal of Cognitive Education and Psychology, 11*(2), 196–208.

Jetton, T. L., & Shanahan, C. (2012). *Adolescent Literacy in the Academic Disciplines: General Principles and Practical Strategies.* New York: Guilford.

Kerbel, D. (2021). *Fred & Marjorie: A Doctor, a Dog, and the Discovery of Insulin.* Toronto: OwlKids.

Kintsch, W. (1988). The Role of Knowledge in Discourse Comprehension: A Construction -Integration Model. *Psychological Review, 95*(2), 163.

Kintsch, W. (1998). *Comprehension: A Paradigm for Cognition.* Cambridge: Cambridge University Press.

Klein, G., & Dabney, A. (2013). *The Cartoon Introduction to Statistics.* New York: Hill and Wang.

Koellner, K., Wallace, F. H., & Swackhamer, L. (2009). Integrating Literature to Support Mathematics Learning in Middle School. *Middle School Journal, 41*(2), 30–9.

Kojima, H., Togami, S., et al. (2009). *The Manga Guide to Calculus.* San Francisco: No Starch Press.

Latta, S., & Weigel, J. (2017). *Smash!: Exploring the Mysteries of the Universe with the Large Hadron Collider.* Minneapolis: Graphic Universe.

Lemire, J., & Walta, G. (2019). *Sentient.* Los Angeles: TKO Studios.

Leonard, M., & Derry, S. J. (2011). What's the Science Behind It? The Interaction of Engineering and Science Goals, Knowledge, and Practices in a Design-Based Science Activity. WCEr Working Paper No. 2011-5. Wisconsin Center for Educational Research. University of WIsconsin-Madison.

Lim, Y. (2019). The Effects of a Comic Book Reading Program on Korean Proficiency and Acculturalization of Youth with an Immigration Background. *Biblia: Journal of the Korean Society for Library and Information Science, 30*(1), 5–27.

Lo-Fo-Wong, D., Beijaerts, A., deHaes, H., & Sprangers, M. (2014). Cancer in Full Color: Use of a Graphic Novel to Identify Distress in Women with Breast Cancer. *Journal of Health Psychology, 19*(12), 1554–63.

McCloud, S. (1993). *Understanding Comics: The Invisible Art.* New York: Harper Perennial.

McCullough, D. (1972). *The Great Bridge.* Simon & Schuster. ISBN 978-0-671-21213-1.

Meier, J. J. (2012). Science Graphic Novels for Academic Libraries: Collections and Collaborators. *College and Research Libraries News, 73*(11), n.p.

Mejia, J. A., Drake, D., & Wilson-Lopez, A. (2015). Changes in Latino/a Adolescents' Engineering Self-efficacy and Perceptions of Engineering after Addressing Authentic Engineering Design Challenges. *122nd ASEE Annual Conference, June 14–17, 2015. Seattle, WA.* (Paper ID# 13238)

Meyer, C. K., & Jimenez, L. M. (2017). Using Every Word and Image: Framing Graphic Novel Instruction in the Expanded Four Resources Model. *Journal of Adolescent and Adult Literacy, 61*(2), 153–61.

Minstrell, J., & Kraus, P. (2005). Guided Inquiry in the Science Classroom. In John D. Bransford and S. Donovan, *How Students Learn: History, Mathematics, and Science in the Classroom* (pp. 475–513). Washington D.C.: The National Academies Press.

Moeller, R. A. (2008). *"No Thanks, these are Boy Books": A Feminist Cultural Analysis of Graphic Novels as Curricular Materials* (Dissertation). Proquest.

Moeller, R. A. (2011). Aren't those Boy Books?: High School Students' Readings of Gender in Graphic Novels. *Journal of Adolescent and Adult Literacy, 54*, 476–84.

Monnin, K. M. (2008). *Perceptions of New Literacies with the Graphic Novel Bone* (Dissertation). Kent State University.

Moore, A. (1986). *Watchmen*. New York: DC Comics.

Moore, A., & Gibbons, D. (2019). *The Watchmen*. New York: DC.

Mosco, R., & Chad, J. (2018). *Science Comics: Solar System: Our Place in Space*. New York: First Second.

Moss, M. (2017). *Last Things*. San Francisco: Conari Press.

National Center for Education Statistics (2015). *National Assessment of Educational Progress (NAEP)*. Washington D.C.: US Department of Education.

Nesmith, S., Cooper, S., & Schwartz, G. (2011). Exploring Graphic Novels for Elementary Science and Mathematics. *School Library Research, 14*, 1–16.

Nott, D. (2023). *Hidden Systems: Water, Electricity, the Internet, and the Secrets Behind the Systems We Use Everyday*. New York: Abrams Comic Arts.

Onesto, A. (2022). *The Ella Project*. https://www.theellaproject.com/

Ottaviani, J. (2016). *The Imitation Game: Alan Turing Decoded*. New York: Harry Abrams.

Ottaviani, J., Cannon, Z., & Cannon, K. (2009). *T-Minus, Race to the Moon*. New York: Aladdin.

Ottaviani, J., Johnston, J., Lieber, S., Locke, V., Parker, J., Mireault, B., & Kemple, C. (2001). *Fallout: J. Robert Oppenheimer, Leo Szilard, and the Political Science of the Atomic Bomb*. Ann Arbor: G.T. Labs.

Ottaviani, J., & Myrick, L. (2011). *Feynman*. New York: First Second.

Ottaviani, J., & Myrick, L. (2019). *Hawking*. New York: First Second.

Ottaviani, J., & Purvis, L. (2016). *The Imitation Game: Alan Turing Decoded*. New York: Abrams Comic Arts.

Ottaviani, J., Purvis, L., Hosler, J., Langridge, R., Leialuha, S., Medley, L., & Parker, J. ([2004] 2009). *Suspended in Language: Niels Bohr's Life, Discoveries, and the Century He Shaped*. Ann Arbor: G.T. Labs.

Ottaviani, J., & Wicks, M. (2013). *Primates: The Fearless Science of Jane Goodall, Dian Fossey, and Birute Galdikas*. New York: First Second.

Ottaviani, J., & Wicks, M. (2020). *Astronauts: Women on the Final Frontier*. New York: First Second.

Oz, H., & Efecioglu, E. (2015). Graphic Novels: An Alternative Approach to Teach English as a Foreign Language. *Journal of Language and Linguistic Studies, 11*(1), 75–90.

Padua, S. (2015). *The Thrilling Adventures for Lovelace and Babbage*. New York: Penguin.

Royal, D. P. (2012). Drawing Attention: Comics as a Means of Approaching US Cultural Diversity. In L. Dong, *Teaching Comics and Graphic Narratives: Essay on Theory, Strategy and Practice* (pp. 67–79). Jefferson: McFarland and Company.

Sabeti, S. (2012). Reading Graphic Novels in School: Texts, Contexts, and the Interpretive Work of Critical Reading. *Pedagogy, Culture, and Society, 20*(2), 191–210.

Schultz, M., Cannon, Z., & Cannon, K. (2009). *The Stuff of Life: A Graphic Guide to Genetics and DNA.* New York: Hill and Wang.

Scott, M., & Chobot, J. (2018). *Robots and Drones: Past, Present and Future.* New York: First Second.

Shanahan, C. (2012). Learning with Text in Science. In Tamara Jetton & Cynthia Shanahan, *Adolescent Literacy in the Academic Disciplines: General Principles and Practical Strategies.* New York: Guilford.

Shanahan, T., & Shanahan, C. (2008). Teaching Disciplinary Literacy to Adolescents: Rethinking Content Area Literacy. *Harvard Educational Review, 78*(1), 40–59.

Siebert, D., & Draper, R. J. (2012). Reconceptualizing Literacy and Instruction for Mathematics Classrooms. In T. L. Jetton & C. Shanahan, *Adolescent Literacy in the Academic Disciplines: General Principles and Practical Strategies* (pp. 172–98). New York: Guilford.

Small, D. (2009). *Stitches: A Memoir.* New York: W.W. Norton.

Snow, M., & Robbins, M. (2015). How Should We Remember the Alamo?: Critical Analysis of Four Graphic Novels. *Social Studies Research and Practice, 10*(2), n.p.

Stephens, G. (2015). Unveiling Cultural Filters: Teaching "The Veil" in Puerto Rico and Saudi Arabia. *Studies in English Language Teaching, 3*(1), 83–100.

Takahashi, S. (2008). *The Manga Guide to Statistics.* San Francisco: No Starch Press.

Takahashi, S., Inoue, I. et al. (2012). *The Manga Guide to Linear Algebra.* San Francisco: No Starch Press.

Takahashi, S., Inoue, I. et al. (2016). *The Manga Guide to Regression Analysis.* San Francisco: No Starch Press.

Tatalovic, M. (2009). Science Comics are Tools for Science Education and Communication: A Brief, Exploratory Study. *Journal of Science Education, 8*(4), 1–17.

Tatsuta, K. (2017). *Ichi-F.* Tokyo: Kodansha Comics.

Telgemeier, R. (2019). *Guts.* New York: Scholastic.

The Ella Project. *Elle the Engineer Comic Books.* https://www.theellaproject.com/deloitte-ella-comic-books

Thielbar, M., & Helmer, D. (2010). *The Kung Fu Puzzle: A Mystery with Time and Temperature.* Minneapolis: Graphic Universe.

Thielbar, M., & Ota, Y. (2010). *The Secret Ghost: A Mystery with Distance and Measurement.* Minneapolis: Graphic Universe.

Thielbar, M., & Pantoja, T. (2011). *The Ancient Formula: A Mystery with Fractions.* Minneapolis: Graphic Universe.

Tomasi, P. J., & Duvall, T. (2018). *The Bridge: How the Roeblings Connected Brooklyn to New York.* New York: Abrams ComicArts.

Tufte, E. (2001). *The Visual Display of Quantitative Information* (2nd ed.). Cheshire: Graphics Press LLC.

UK Department of Education (2019, November). *School Workforce Census.* Retrieved from https://explore-education-statistics.service.gov.uk/find-statistics/school-workforce-in-england

Vandermeersche, G., & Soetaert, R. (2011). Intermediality as Cultural Literacy and Teaching the Graphic Novel. *CLC Web: Comparative Literature and Culture, 13*(3), 20.

Warden, E. (2022). Problem Posing through Young Adult Literature. *Mathematics Teacher: Learning and Teaching PK-12, 115*(7), 453–89.

Wicks, M. (2015). *Human Body Theater*. New York: First Second.

Wilgus, B. A., & Brooks, M. (2017). *Science Comics: Flying Machines*. New York: First Second.

Wilson, E. O., Ottaviani, J., & Butzer, C. M. (2020). *Naturalist: A Graphic Adaptation*. Washington D.C.: Island Press.

Wilson-Lopez, A., Strong, A. R., Hartman, C., Garlick, J., Washburn, K., Minichiello, A., Weingart, S., & Acosta-Feliz, J. (2020). A Systematic Review of Argumentation Related to the Engineering World. *Journal of Engineering Education, 109*, 281–306.

Winick, J. (2000). *Pedro and Me: Friendship, Loss, and What I Learned*. New York: Henry Holt.

Wolsey, T. D., Lapp, D., Grant, M. C., & Karkouti, I. M. (2019). Intersections of Literacy and Teaching with the Disciplines and Professions: We Asked Some Experts. *Journal of Adolescent and Adult Literacy, 63*(3), 251–6.

Wong, S., Miao, H., Cheng, R., & Yip, M. (2017). Graphic Novel Comprehension among Learners with Differential Cognitive Styles and Reading Abilities. *Reading and Writing Quarterly, 33*(4), 412–27.

Wood, M. (2015). *The Effect of Graphic Novel Supplements on Reading Comprehension and Motivation in Secondary Students* (Dissertation). Proquest.

Wright, W. (1902). *Some Aeronautical Experiments from the Smithsonian*. Government Printing Office. [Manuscript/Mixed Material] Retrieved from the Library of Congress, https://www.loc.gov/item/wright002972/.

Yahgulanaas, M. (2019). *Carpe Fin*. Vancouver: Douglas & Macintyre.

Yang, G. L., & Holmes, M. (2015). *Secret Coders*. New York: First Second.

Yang, G. L., & Holmes, M. (2016). *Secret Coders: Paths and Portals*. New York: First Second. (Note: This is volume 2 of the six-volume series – all 6 are listed in the appendix).

Yang, G. L., & Holmes, M. (2017). *Secret Coders: Robots and Repeats*. New York: First Second.

Yang, G. L., & Holmes, M. (2018). *Secret Coders: Monsters and Modules*. New York: First Second.

Yang, G. L., & Kim, D. K. (2010). *Prime Baby*. New York: First Second.

Zettwoch, D. (2019). *Science Comics: Cars: Engines That Move You*. New York: First Second.

Zunger, Y. (2018, March 22). Computer Science Faces an Ethics Crisis: The Cambridge Analytics Scandal Proves It. *The Boston Globe*, 22. Retrieved from https://www.bostonglobe.com/ideas/2018/03/22/computer-science-faces-ethics -crisi s-the-cambridge-analytics-scandal-proves/IzaXxl2BsYBtwM4nxezgcP/s tory.html.

INDEX